"*Casting Indra's Net* is an enthralling plea for k
life experiences and her refined theologian mi
a thorough investigation of nonviolence in serv~~..~~
and social harmony. Pithy and wise, *Casting Indra's Net* warms the chill of
our troubling times, softening us into wholeness."

—Ruth King, author of *Mindful of Race: Transforming Racism
from the Inside Out* and Founder of the Mindful of Race Institute

"With clarity and compassion, using powerful storytelling and wise inquiry,
Pamela Ayo Yetunde expertly guides us to understand the indelible truth
of our interconnection as kinship. Carefully and bravely leading us to
comprehend the urgency of our social, political, and environmental crises,
Casting Indra's Net is a poignant cry to release any divisiveness and heed the
call of religious teachings and leaders throughout time that ultimately only
love heals. Weaving together Buddhist practices with Christian and Jewish
parables, Hindu thought, and universal gospel, this book is a compelling and
practical guide for our challenging times."

—Sebene Selassie, author of *You Belong: A Call for Connection*

"Ayo's bravely compassionate book casts us into a net of mutuality—and
brings us up whole. *Casting Indra's Net* invites us to be remade, as by a home-
cooked meal you didn't know you needed, prepared by kin you mistook
for strangers. This book is a gem that mirrors the jeweled possibilities in all
of us."

—Chenxing Han, author of *Be the Refuge:
Raising the Voices of Asian American Buddhists*

"From the depths of our sorrows, Pamela Ayo Yetunde speaks with a prophetic
voice—wise, clear, and passionate. The righteousness she invokes is the call
of love and mutuality rather than warning and wrath. Toward that end, Ayo's

book offers practices to accomplish the oneness of compassion and justice in this very real world we inhabit. We need both."

—Hozan Alan Senauke, author of *Turning Words: Transformative Encounters with Buddhist Teachers* and abbot of Berkeley Zen Center

"Living in a society that is so painfully divided across polarized beliefs, it is all too easy to dismiss folks who hold differing viewpoints and whom we perceive as ignorant or even threatening. In *Casting Indra's Net*, Pamela Ayo Yetunde beautifully reminds us that, in truth, we are interdependent kin, and deep within our cores we have the gifts of respect and compassion to exchange with one another. Weaving together wisdom traditions, especially Buddhism, with the author's penetrating insights and stories, this book offers skillful means for remembering that we are the beloveds of all sentient beings."

—Jeanine Canty, author of *Returning the Self to Nature: Undoing Our Collective Narcissism and Healing Our Planet*

"Pamela Ayo Yetunde draws on the deep wisdom traditions of Buddhism and the Black experience in America to offer us the truth of mutuality and interdependence the world needs so badly at this time."

—Melvin McLeod, Editor-in-Chief, *Lion's Roar*

"Ayo's offering is anchored in her own human story and rooted in her interpretations of Buddhist tradition and astute analysis of our present politics. With her book's two core images (drawn from ancient stories) of all of our souls as interconnected nodes in a vast cosmic net, and the garlands of fragrant flowers or bloody fingers that we make for ourselves as each of our actions contributes to mutuality or to mobbery, Ayo weaves an authentic invitation to all of us to draw on her reflection and teaching—and on the stories and practices each of us has inherited, lived, and encountered—

to be our most fully present and compassionate selves, in kinship with all beings. *Casting Indra's Net* is not meant to live in its pages—it is an offering of orientation and practice, asking all of us to live into the world Ayo envisions and invites us to cocreate: This book is already a river with many tributaries, with Ayo's ancestors in thought and practice alive and with her in its pages. Where it will go depends on how we, her readers, answer her question, 'What part do you want to play?'"

—Rabbi Emma Kippley-Ogman, Associate Chaplain for Jewish Life, Macalester College

"Thank you, Ayo Yetunde, for writing this book! The jewel of your perspective sees with nuance, care, and clear knowing of the potential for all of us to see more fully. This is a call for the committed work of civility. Through touching personal stories, letters, and practices, we are invited to move, to act, to reflect, and to remember how to lean in to support the good that we know is in each of us."

—Peace Twesigye, Assistant Director of Buddhist Studies and the Thich Nhat Hanh Program for Engaged Buddhism at Union Theological Seminary

BOOKS BY PAMELA AYO YETUNDE

Black and Buddhist: What Buddhism Can Teach Us about Race, Resilience, Transformation, and Freedom, coedited with Cheryl A. Giles (Shambhala Publications, 2020)

Buddhist-Christian Dialogue, U.S. Law, and Womanist Theology for Transgender Spiritual Care (Palgrave Macmillan, 2020)

Object Relations, Buddhism, and Relationality in Womanist Practical Theology (Palgrave Macmillan, 2018)

Vigil: Spiritual Reflections on Your Money and Sanity (Marabella Books, 2011)

The Inheritance: A Stock-Picking Story (Marabella Books, 2000)

Beyond 40 Acres and Another Pair of Shoes: For Smart Sisters Who Think Too Much and Do Too Little About Their Money (Marabella Books, 1998)

Casting Indra's Net

FOSTERING SPIRITUAL KINSHIP AND COMMUNITY

Wisdom from Buddhism, Christianity,
Judaism, Hinduism, and more

PAMELA AYO YETUNDE

FOREWORD BY RESMAA MENAKEM
AFTERWORD BY EBOO PATEL

SHAMBHALA

Shambhala Publications, Inc.
2129 13th Street
Boulder, Colorado 80302
www.shambhala.com

Cover art: Nina_FOX/Shutterstock
Cover design: Kate E. White
Interior design: Greta D. Sibley

9 8 7 6 5 4 3 2 1

First Edition
Printed in Canada

Shambhala Publications makes every effort to print on acid-free, recycled paper.
Shambhala Publications is distributed worldwide
by Penguin Random House, Inc., and its subsidiaries.

Library of Congress Cataloging-in-Publication Data
Names: Yetunde, Pamela Ayo, author.
Title: Casting Indra's net: fostering spiritual kinship and community/
Pamela Ayo Yetunde; foreword by Resmaa Menakem; afterword by Eboo Patel.
Description: Boulder: Shambhala, 2023.
Identifiers: LCCN 2022026467 | ISBN 9781645470922 (trade paperback)
Subjects: LCSH: Empathy—Religious aspects. | Spirituality.
Classification: LCC BF575.E55 Y48 2023 | DDC 152.4/1—dc23/eng/20220715
LC record available at https://lccn.loc.gov/2022026467

Contents

Foreword by Resmaa Menakem ix

Preface xii

Acknowledgments xvi

Introduction 1
Finding Our Place in the Network of Mutuality

1. The Suffering of Mobbery 25

2. Beyond the Golden Rule 44
Treating Others as They Need to Be Treated

3. The Four Noble Truths as a Path of
Mutuality and Relationality 60

4. "Say What?" 77
Koans as Relational Wholeworking in Stories of Jesus,
the Canaanite Woman, and Angulimala

5. The Book of Job 96
Self-actualization through Community

6. Action without Attachment 115
The Bhagavad Gita and the Lessons of Paradox

7. Knowing Your Place in the Cosmos 143

8. Letters from a Chicago Condo 167
To Rev. Dr. Martin Luther King Jr. and to My Buddhist Kin

Conclusion 204
Civility as Spiritual Practice and Public Pastoral Care

Afterword by Eboo Patel 213

Notes 215

About the Author 219

Foreword

Gold into Platinum

Welcome to your body, to your human beingness, and to the field of existence.

Welcome to your kinship with all humanity.

Welcome to the ongoing challenge of transforming the interpersonal into the communal.

Welcome to the alchemical process of turning the gold that is you into the platinum that is us.

Welcome to the ever-emerging opportunity to build a community of healing and mutuality.

By now you may have intuited that *Casting Indra's Net* is not just a book. It is a deeply compassionate tour of our interbeing—and a clear and vibrant call to live into it. It is a call that, once heard, must be either followed or deliberately ignored.

As Sibling Ayo reminds us over and over, we are all kin. We all have some of the same mitochondria as our Great Mother, a woman who lived in southern Africa about 200,000 years ago.

We all also share the same bigger body. Our human bodies all come from the same source and the same elements—elements that, in many cases, are also found in stars.

This bigger body—Indra's Net—creates our inescapable mutuality. It also creates an ever-present, all-important challenge, which Sibling Ayo articulates brilliantly:

> We were conceived into the Net, born into it, and exist within it. We will die in its entanglements. In the meantime, can we enhance the ways we live in this vast and abundant community of kin, near and far?

Sibling Ayo offers us a twelve-part process to help us live up to and into this challenge. This process, which she calls the Platinum Rule, transmutes a simple recognition of our inescapable mutuality into ongoing discernment, wise engagement, and what Ayo calls *wholeworking*.

Sibling Ayo's Platinum Rule stands on the shoulders of the Golden Rule, recognizing both its virtues and its limitations—and then seeing beyond it, into dimensions of our lives that the Golden Rule simply cannot reach. (There has been at least one earlier version of a Platinum Rule formulated by other folks—but, like the Golden Rule, it falls short of genuine mutuality.) Ayo's Platinum Rule beautifully embodies *ma'at*, which is a word from the Kemetic tradition that means *what is just, true, and righteous*.

The twentieth-century Catholic mystic Thomas Merton once reflected, *There is no way of telling people that they are all walking around shining like the sun.* After an experience of awakening, Gotama (the seventh-century B.C.E. sage whom we now usually call the Buddha) had a similar thought. Then they both got over it. Eventually, each recognized and worked creatively to build and sustain community.

So does Sibling Ayo, who reminds and challenges us, again and again, *Why not be the shining star you really are?*

Casting Indra's Net calls us to live out of—and into—the best parts of who we are. Because we are all kin, Sibling Ayo urges us to return to our basic goodness and choose mutuality over brutality time after time, moment after moment, breath upon breath.

If you're ready to be part of this transmutation, please turn the page.

—Resmaa Menakem, author of *My Grandmother's Hands,*
The Quaking of America, and *Monsters in Love*

Preface

I am an activist, Buddhist lay leader, chaplain, pastoral counselor, practical theologian, and teacher. In these various roles, I have witnessed hatred, destruction, defensiveness, illness, and ignorance. I have also seen love, compassion, insight, recovery, and enlightenment. What concerns me the most is how our obviously changeable values and ethical obligations are constantly politically exploited in order to violently turn us against one another. What is being exploited? The suffering of insignificance and the clinging to entitlement. More about this later. I am concerned that humanity's greatest threat is the distortion of our humanity. When I use the word "humanity," I mean you, me, and us. I'm writing this book for all of us.

Let's take the example of our contrasting responses to the common cold and to COVID-19. According to a 2008 study in the *Journal of General Virology*, the common cold virus may have come from birds over two hundred years ago. Although we could not see the virus, over time, humans accepted its existence and learned anyone could catch it because it is airborne. We agreed that if we had a cold, we did not want to pass it along to anyone. If one had a cold and felt a sneeze coming on, one could turn one's head, take a step back, cover one's mouth, sneeze, and say, "Excuse me," and others would say in response, "God bless you" or "*Gezondheid.*" We cared enough about others to shield them from the relatively benign common cold and wish them well on their journey to health.

Such willingness stands in stark contrast to our failure to stem the spread of the deadly COVID-19 virus. Many people who accepted the reality of the common cold and the flu denied COVID-19's existence and its effects—some even while on their deathbeds, dying of the virus! Many patients and their families abused medical professionals, especially nurses, who valiantly treated these patients. Many, in a show of defiance against what they perceived as state intrusion into their bodies, refused to wear masks, refused to engage in social distancing, and refused vaccination. Even some first responders protested against vaccine mandates. COVID-19 grew from epidemic to pandemic to endemic in part because the virus was politicized and racialized, and public health experts were minimized and undermined. Millions of people worldwide were infected and died. This period in history will have long-lasting psychological effects on every community on every continent on this planet. What will be our plan for resilience?

Out of polite customs borne from a sense of mutuality, we did our best to protect ourselves and others from the cold and flu and treated those with a cold or flu with concern, yet tens of millions of us risked being exposed to COVID-19 and transmitting it to others. That choice was irrational and brutal. What happened to us? Why did many of us choose brutality over mutuality? None of this makes sense unless we understand that there has been a persistent and devastating devaluing of civility that puts us all at risk. Why is the cultivation and maintenance of civility vital? Because the opposite is brutish. As a pastoral counselor, chaplain, and spiritual director, I often hear my clients ask some version of the question, "What is my purpose?" I know deep in my heart and in my bone marrow that each one of us shares one baseline purpose—to keep in check our animalistic tendencies to preemptively attack perceived enemies. Today, each one of us is being invited to do just the opposite—to unleash the animal in us on another. I beg you on bended knee to reject that invitation.

I believe our truest, purest, healthiest nature is to care for humans who cannot care for themselves. The recognition of human vulnerability often evokes a compassionate response if we aren't distracted and deluded. Yet such distraction and delusion always remain possibilities due to our cultural conditionings and our evolutionary fight, flight, or freeze instincts, so it takes practice to return again and again to our healthiest nature. In Buddhism, we call this truest, purest state of being our original face, compassion, basic goodness, or Buddhanature. In Christianity, we say that the example of Jesus's life was all about helping those in need and teaching others to do the same. In Hinduism, we reflect on the story of Arjuna contemplating the meaning of service in the midst of conflicting moral dilemmas. In Islam, we consider how to put mercy, service, and prayer into practice. In Judaism, we are encouraged to fix a broken world. In Taoism, we ponder how all that exists has its opposite, with all things in dynamic relationship with one another. From each of these religions, I draw the lesson that being in dynamic relationship with our "opposite" is a key skill to our survival, lest we continue on the path of destroying people we don't like because their existence reminds us of our own vulnerability. It is so easy to operate out of this falsehood.

If we don't embrace civility now, the children we bring into this world will stand little chance of having a life conducive to their full flourishing. Hopefully, we haven't irretrievably stooped so low as to not be able to care for our offspring, but even that is in question. It is with this thought that I want to introduce the practice of contemplation in this book's preface.

"Contemplation" means to focus one's thinking processes on something so as to penetrate its deeper meaning. We do this to be better informed of the true nature of this phenomenon or noumenon (something that exists but is not detectable through our senses), to better understand our relationship to this reality, and to accept it for what it is. In doing so, we manage our anxiety about both it and ourselves. We contemplate by removing distractions or moving ourselves to a place with fewer distractions so we can just think deeply about this reality. Contemplation is aided by paying attention to our body postures and breath and regulating the body and breath when we feel the discomfort and anxiety that may arise in contemplating something we have difficulty accepting. For example, if you are contemplating wisdom teachings on forgiveness, and a memory arises about a relationship you want to mend but have too much resentment about to make the first move, you may feel tension in your body and your breathing may become shallow or more rapid. Yet given your devotion to deepening love and wisdom—perhaps in the form of Jesus, Buddha, another religious figure, or simply your own heart's ideal—you remain committed to the contemplation by regulating your body and breath so you can keep your attention there. I invite you to read this entire book as a contemplation. Take your good, sweet time with it.

Acknowledgments

There are countless known and unknown beings who have contributed to the causes and conditions for the publication of this book. The recognition of this fact inspired me to try to capture my feelings of awe and appreciation in a poem.

i was pushed

        through my mother's

        bloody lei and

placed

        in a bed

        of flowers

            in a garden in the sky

        tendrils of rain-tear descending droplets

quenching dry deserts of daddy's thirst

for another African daisy, tulip, lily, viola, iris, and hollyhock

to be planted

in the cosmic flower bed

for a variegated garland

to be stitched

with a blood-red thread of

petals iridescent in Sol's rainbow sheen

and also

opaque by mud-blunted ignorance

P-A-R-A-D-O-X

roots

stunted by

parched-cracked soil, but only in that season's drought and

Sol casts another rainbow sheen and red dew drops

D

.

R

.

O

.

P

stalks sprout!

The ultimate in radical kinship

is

    The Way

    The Great I Am

    The Tagathata

    Allah and

    Om

        elements for survival and

i have survived and thrived

in

                INDRA'S NET!

Thank you

Tracey Scott for your love

Matt Zepelin for your scouting and scalpel

Gerry Shishin Wick for *The Book of Equanimity*

Sosan Theresa Flynn for your leadership and koan study group

John Chang-Yee Lee for your honesty and kinship

Alisha Tatem for our pastoral counseling journey and your creativity

Ben Connelly for your passion for people and sutras

Satyani McPherson for your clarity and care

Jessi LeClear-Vachta for your hospitality and interfaith commitments

Peter Schumacher for your skillfulness and reinforcement

AJ Johnston for your white awareness leadership and racial reckoning

Gina Sharpe for your guidance and introducing me to *Lion's Roar*

Melvin McLeod for publishing "Buddhism in the Age of Black Lives Matter"

Barbara Holmes for reading "Buddhism in the Age of Black Lives Matter" and contacting me

Sharon Tan and the faculty at United Theological Seminary of the Twin Cities in 2016 for hiring me to direct their Interreligious Chaplaincy program 2017–2020

The chaplaincy students in my classes for their commitment to inter-religious spiritual care competency

Larry Yang for *Awakening Together*, the book and practice, and keeping me in your imagination;

Shambhala Publications for its mission and investment

Resmaa Menakem for your depth and courage

Eboo Patel for your vision and perseverance

Zenzele Isoke for your true sistership and artistry

PB for acceptance and justice

Scott Edelstein for your wisdom and insistence

Everyone who endorsed this book

Everyone I forgot to mention and

You. Yes, you, my spiritual kin.

The topics in this book are of a very serious nature, so here's a koan in appreciation and preparation.

Trayshawn, the weekly housekeeper, was sweeping a heap of fallen red maple leaves off the balcony onto the sidewalk while neighbor Cam was walking their enormous English Mastiff. The leaves, with the help of an unexpected breeze, fell onto Cam and the dog. Cam shouted at Trayshawn, "Watch it! How dare you sweep your dirty leaves on your neighbors!" The dog whined and chased its tail. Trayshawn stopped and said, "You're right. I'm so sorry. Wait right there." Cam stopped, then gave the dog his triple-decker cheeseburger for comfort. Trayshawn grabbed a bucket of water, gathered the remaining leaves into a pile on the balcony, dumped them in the bucket, washed them, dumped them back onto the balcony, and began sweeping the soggy pile onto Cam and the dog, saying, "Having washed the leaves, now I see." Cam, humiliated and infuriated, screamed, "I said watch it, not wash it! And what do you mean by 'You see'? You can't even hear!" Cam's great mastiff, aggravated by the friction and the burger, shat a huge, hot load on the pile of washed leaves, creating an odor that wafted upward to Trayshawn. "I may not be able to hear, and I may not see all that well, but I sure can smell!" "Oh yeah, and what is that you smell?" Trayshawn paused, searched the sky, opened his mouth, and said, "Woof, woof!" The dog barked back, and Cam, bringing hands into prayer pose, fell to his knees in reverence to scoop the poop.

Introduction

Finding Our Place in the Network of Mutuality

And don't forget in doing something for others that you have what you have because of others. Don't forget that. We are tied together in life and in the world. And you may think you got all you got by yourself. But you know, before you got out here to church this morning, you were dependent on more than half of the world. You get up in the morning and go to the bathroom, and you reach over for a bar of soap, and that's handed to you by a Frenchman. You reach over for a sponge, and that's given to you by a Turk. You reach over for a towel, and that comes to your hands from the hands of a Pacific Islander. And then you go on to the kitchen to get your breakfast. You reach on over to get a little coffee, and that's poured in your cup by a South American. Maybe you decide that you want a little tea this morning, only to discover that that's poured in your cup by a Chinese. Or maybe you want a little cocoa, that's poured in your cup by a West African. Then you want a little bread and you reach over to get it, and that's

given to you by the hands of an English-speaking farmer, not to
mention the baker. Before you get through eating breakfast in the
morning, you're dependent on more than half the world. That's
the way God structured it. . . . So let us be concerned about others
because we are dependent on others.[1]

—Martin Luther King Jr.

It has been some sixty years since Martin Luther King Jr. shared his
message that we—each of us—rely on the rest of the world, but today,
many of us in the United States are wondering with a jagged edge of
insecurity, anger, and rage, "Does the world also rely on us?" In this I
detect the lingering entitlement of the era of American imperialism.
How remarkable that this man, who at that very moment was feared
and hated by so many in his own country, had the awareness to
affirm our mutual interconnectedness. And his awareness was also a
kind of clarion call for global awareness and positive regard, as our
economic situation has only become more globalized since the time
of his writing. The transformation of manufacturing towns to notches
on the American Rust Belt, the offshoring of jobs, the rise of other
nations' economies, the mass movements of peoples within and between nations, the Internet—these and so many other developments
have led to our current situation in which King's message resonates
strongly, as do messages such as "Make America Great Again" that
invoke love and care as well as underlying shame and entitlement. A
strange mix of patriotism and nationalism.

Do we see our economic situation and predicament as a chance to
practice gratitude and dialogue, or do we mostly let it stoke our resentment and anger? And for those of us who have thus far done well in
the globalized economy—do we truly see the humanity of those in our

communities who are suffering from economic inequality, or do we think of them as underserved or ignorant and separate ourselves from them? In our affluence, do we support systems that keep inventive and industrious people trapped in the stunted stage that the developmental psychologist Erik Erikson called "industry vs. inferiority"? By this, I mean perpetuating social and economic systems that prevent workers from realizing their true capacities and thus consistently frustrate them and leave them feeling inferior. In our economic interconnectedness and real or perceived vulnerability, we are all subject to the rage of our rageful political leaders once they have ascended to the top of the political structure and the free press is obligated to provide coverage. We have choices about how we will react and respond, and many of the events in recent years have not been encouraging in this regard.

This book is a plea. I'm virtually on my hands and knees begging—it brings The Temptations' 1966 song "Ain't Too Proud to Beg" to mind. Their song is about the romantic love between a man desperate for love and the woman, his sweet darlin', who is about to leave him. My pleading and begging are not about romance but are the heartfelt expression of an older black woman, arguably now an elder, with a familial love for all, irrespective of gender, race, sexuality, and various expressions of identity. As the daughter of a mother who was adopted and as the mother of my adopted child, by "familial" I mean seeing each other as kin and leaning into a posture toward adopting each other as relatives. Watching those committing violence through mobbery—a term and phenomenon I describe in chapter 1—who are depriving us of the opportunity to realize and express our genuine kinship, I beg and plead with you all, sweet darlins, because I refuse to let you go. Please stay with me in the fold of love and civility, 'cause I ain't too proud to beg.

Elsewhere in his "Letter from Birmingham Jail" (1963), King offered the beautiful image of "the inescapable network of our mutuality." These words came from the thinking of a Christian, but you won't find them in the Bible. Where did this inescapable network concept come from? Given that King studied the Hindu social activist Mohandas K. Gandhi, the theologian in me sees an embedded Vedic cosmology, anthropology, and philosophy within King's Christian message. In ancient Vedic thought, the inescapable network is called Indra's Net. The imagery is of a net that spans the universe, and each node within the net is a jewel that reflects all the other jewels. It is a metaphor for the way that all of life is interconnected—we are mirrors, diamonds, and pearls in this flowing, universal net.

The Indra's Net concept was richly elaborated on in the Avatamsaka, or Flower Ornament Scripture, one of the most influential sutras of East Asian Buddhism, and it forms the cosmology of the Huayen or Flower Garland school of the religion. The "mutuality" in King's vision and in the vision of Indra's Net comes from the belief that we are all made of the same substances, each substance being porous, changeable, impermanent, empty, and interpenetrating. This recognition is part of the process of "casting" the net by expanding our consciousness and heart's capacity toward radical inclusivity. Net-casting is also a central motif in Christianity; Jesus asked his disciples to cast their net to catch the fish needed to sustain themselves. In doing so, they caught more fish than the net should have been able to hold. The lesson? Net-casting for the benefit of the whole returns what already exists—wholeness. This story has been used to support prosperity gospel theologies that espouse the acquisition of material goods, but I would rather focus on the net-casting process because of what it can allow us to be toward one another. Casting Indra's Net supports the resplendent cosmology of mutuality.

Mutuality is the reality of our cosmos and our being, and it can form the philosophical ground for our ethics. But this truth becomes obscured by the delusion that religious differences, geopolitical grasping, political power plays, and so on are the substance of our reality. In the service of creating a civil society, our task as nodal jewels is to reflect, with as little distortion as possible, our mutuality. Otherwise, we run the risk that our perceptions and reflections will create monstrous images to fear and destroy.

———

On May 25, 2020, the unarmed black man George Floyd was tortured by police for nearly ten minutes in broad daylight in front of witnesses who pleaded for the intentional choking to stop as they recorded the heinous arrest. This brutal murder was recorded on several cell phones and store cameras and, as the videos were posted online, they spread virally. People around the United States and the world responded with the shock to our collective conscience—the textbook definition of what happens when we know a human rights abuse has occurred. It is an "Oh, my God!" or "What the f—k!" expression of shock, eventually followed by the thought that something has to change. Some of us responded in dignified ways while others responded with violence against individuals and property that had no relationship to the murder.

At the time, I lived in St. Paul, Minnesota, just several miles from the site of this international human rights atrocity. A few days later I traveled to Chicago because I had already planned a trip to visit family. I remember being in a high-rise apartment in downtown Chicago. A peaceful protest that day was followed by an evening of angry people smashing store windows, entering, and stealing. The US president warned in a tweet on May 29 that "when the looting starts, the shooting starts"—a saying that has been used by racist politicians and police officers to quell civil rights protestors in different decades and different places. I remember watching the underbelly of helicopters, hearing the protestors, and seeing plumes of black smoke rising from a burning vehicle. I stayed inside.

On the following day, I attempted to venture around the corner for a bite to eat. When I exited, I looked in both directions and saw that the block was surrounded by several clusters of police officers. There I was, a black person in close proximity to about twenty officers. My body tensed up as if my head and feet were being pulled in opposite directions by a string as long as the history of police brutality against black people. Making my way toward the corner, I saw what seemed like hundreds of police officers marching in formation. Was this Chicago, Illinois, USA? What was happening to our First Amendment rights to free speech and assembly? Could those rights only be exercised under police watch to prevent violent outbreaks? It felt to me like what I'd seen in the broadcasts of police crackdowns on activists in Hong Kong as they assembled to defy China's takeover or reintegration (depending on your point of view), or some other police state. I presumed the militarized police force was marching toward a political protest against the kind of police brutality that killed George Floyd and countless other unarmed black people before him. I went back into the building. Sitting in a glass-encased studio apartment twenty-seven stories up, I listened to the helicopters, observed their underbellies, and watched the smoke billowing up, and I felt no aversion to it. I practiced a meditation called *tonglen*, in which one first imagines intentionally breathing in smoke or clouds and breathing them out, which is a way of preparing one's body, mind, and heart to then breathe in one's own or others' suffering before breathing out the relief from that suffering. I imagined breathing in the dark smoke for the benefit of others. Being with my breath, mind, and heart in this way, I felt at one with the rage while not wanting to behave in an enraged way. I understood the rage that was being expressed on the streets, though my own felt rage was eventually expressed as empathy, then action.

Eventually, the shock to my conscience, combined with reflecting on the Buddhist archetype Avalokiteshvara (the one who hears the cries of the world and acts skillfully), led me to help create Buddhist Justice Reporter (BJR).[2] BJR was founded by Buddhists who are people of color and also writers. We began writing about the prosecution of the police who tortured and killed George Floyd. BJR was launched with the generous support of *Tricycle: The Buddhist Review* and is supported by Common Ground Meditation Center, an Insight Meditation community in Minneapolis, Minnesota; the Kataly Foundation; *Lion's Roar*; and many individual supporters. In addition to writing about the trial of the police officer who violated Floyd's human rights, resulting in his death, BJR has published articles about other justice issues. Given the rising tide of white supremacist* authoritarianism justified by calls for Christian nationalism, those in radically contemplative religious traditions would do well to consider whether their embrace of silence is being interpreted by others as permission to continue injustice in the name of a twisted religious ideology. It is time for us to speak up.

I tell the above story as a way of asking: How can we empathize with acute mass suffering without getting swept up in acts of mass

---

* I intend to eventually renounce the term "white supremacy" for something more complex. In later chapters of this book, I use and explore terms such as "white existential aggravation," "white existential angst," and "white existential paranoia."

violence? Is it time for a compassion *revolution*? If we are to have any chance of creating such a revolution, I know it must begin with courageously facing ourselves and each other. If our compassion bypasses what we find most difficult, we will not develop the strength to weather our most profound challenges. This is the topic we'll be exploring together throughout this book, and I want to begin with my own story. My ability to both understand the rage that followed George Floyd's murder and channel it constructively did not appear out of nowhere. There was a time when I had difficulty facing the reality of death at all.

Learning to Face Living and Dying

I was born in 1961, the first of two children born to working-class African American parents, a cisgender man and woman, in Indiana, where I lived the first third of my life. As a Christian family, we religiously went to church on Sunday mornings. At home, we prayed before we ate and at night before going to sleep. We listened to gospel music and were taught to believe in God and to enact lives of service. Part of being in community was to be ready to offer support should anyone ever be in need. We took communion monthly and were taught never to question the teachings in the Bible because the Bible was the inerrant word of God—the omniscient, omnipotent, jealous, and loving Father of us all who would also damn his disobedient children to hell forever. I didn't really buy that part of the God talk because I actually had a loving father, the man married to my mother. Their marriage lasted only ten years because he died suddenly of cardiac arrest at the age of thirty-five, doing what he loved doing, playing golf. I was only eight years old.

I had never experienced losing someone to death, so I had never been exposed to any rituals around attending to a dead body. I have vague memories of attending the wake for my father. He was given the traditional funeral rituals of the black and United Methodist Church in the United States. I saw his motionless and ashen body in a casket. I was in shock, and when the time for his funeral came a few days later, I refused to go. I faked having a stomachache. It had already been established after I stole money from my brother that I was not a good liar, so my mother must have known I was faking, and she allowed me not to go to the funeral.

Between the ages of eight and thirty-nine, I attended only three funerals, and each one elicited a different response from me. I chose to attend two of the three funerals specifically because I didn't know the deceased. I thought it would be a good experience for me to overcome my fear of the dead—and of my own biological nature—by accompanying bereaved friends to funerals of people I didn't know. At one funeral, no one cried, and I was able to stuff my emotions down well. At another funeral, I heard only a few sniffles, and I wailed as if I knew the person, loved them, and had just heard of their death. At the third funeral, for one of my beloved aunts, I was inconsolable—the kind of inconsolability that detracts from the funeral service itself. Comparing myself to others, I knew I didn't have a grip on what it means to live a human life, and that was not something I was willing to continue.

It was also during this period of my life that I learned my cousin was dying of AIDS. He wanted to be visited by relatives, and some of the relatives who knew he was dying did not want to be with him. I was aghast. My protective side kicked into gear, and I visited him for four days. A few months later, he died in hospice. I was thirty at the time, and though I did not attend his funeral, this caregiving experience planted a seed deep within me. I learned that I wanted to be able to attend to dying people as I had been able to do for my cousin. Yet I lacked confidence: I still believed, based on the death of my father and my responses to the funerals I had attended, that I was not capable of being with dying people. Nevertheless, I gained a vision for the kind of person I wanted to be. I put that vision deep in the nether regions of my mind and forgot about it as I proceeded to graduate from law school, work as a political asylum officer for what was then known as the Immigration and Naturalization Service, work for the San Francisco Democratic Party, and eventually go into personal finance consulting and writing.

CONTEMPLATION
Touching and Watering Your Seeds and Flowers

I trained as a community dharma leader (CDL) at Spirit Rock Meditation Center, but before I entered and completed this training, I practiced in the Plum Village tradition of the late Vietnamese Zen Master Thich Nhat Hanh (known by his students as Thay). The sanghas I attended were in the Community of Mindful Living (CML). In the CDL training, I learned how to offer meditation in the Insight tradition, and in CML, I learned how Thay reimagined and rearticulated Buddhism through poetic expressions using the natural elements of water and flowers. This practice offers a little from both of these sources. The underlying anthropology is that human beings are made of the same elements as plants and that plant elements and human elements interpenetrate. Please allow at least fifteen minutes for this practice.

———

Bring yourself to a seated position in a place without distractions. Release any object from your hands—phone, pen, keyboard, paper, or anything else. Position your body in such a way that you are comfortable and feel well-supported beneath your feet and at the base of your spine, so that it only takes a subtle effort to remain still and alert. Gently close your eyes and keep them lightly closed. This helps support the visualization in your mind's eye. With an unfocused awareness, notice what's happening in your body. Whatever sensations arise, whatever pressures you feel, whatever is expanding and contracting, notice it, and notice whatever messages arise in your mind about your experience. When you notice those messages as "judgmental," bring a slight smile to your face and silently say to yourself, "Judging." So many of us have been conditioned to be judgmental about ourselves that it is like second nature, but it is not our first nature.

Notice your breath without trying to change it. If your mind carries messages that your breathing should be different than it is, bring another slight smile to your face and say silently to yourself, "Judging." This is how the mind works sometimes, so try not to personalize it. As you breathe in, silently say to yourself, "Breathing in," and as you breathe out, silently say to yourself, "Breathing out." Allow yourself to notice your in-breath and your out-breath for several rounds, then bring to mind the image of a sunflower, and let that image rest in your mind's eye. Say to yourself:

"Breathing in, I am soil; breathing out, I am fertilized. In soil, out fertilized.

Breathing in, I contain sunflower seeds; breathing out, seeds are rooting. In seeds, out roots.

Breathing in, I break through the soil; breathing out, I reveal myself. In breaking, out revealing.

Breathing in, I am more exposed to the elements; breathing out, I thrive. In exposure, out thriving.

Breathing in, my sunflower glory is in brilliant display; breathing out, I am beautiful. In brilliant, out beautiful."

Rest with the visualization, including any feelings, thoughts, and sensations. Take one long in-breath and one long out-breath. Gently open your eyes. If there is no slight smile on your face, bring one to your lips, bring your hands together in prayer/namaste/*gassho* pose, and bow to end your meditation.

It was about ten years after my cousin died that, one otherwise unremarkable workday, my long-latent desire to attend to dying people caught me completely by surprise. I decided to get some rest after a day of stock portfolio trading by not lingering in the office for small talk with colleagues, so I went home to do nothing. Arriving home, I decided to treat myself to *The Oprah Winfrey Show*. It wasn't customary for me to watch her show daily, but something told me that I should watch it that day. On this particular day, Mattie Stepanek was her guest. Mattie was a boy, only eleven years old, born with dysautonomic mitochondrial myopathy, a rare form of muscular dystrophy, and he had spent most of his life in and out of the hospital. Sweet and adorable Mattie was reading from his book of poetry *Heartsongs*.

He told Oprah that when he was hospitalized and feeling up to it, he would wheel his books from room to room to share with the children on his ward. Hearing his words, a thrust of emotion poured through my body like a tsunami. The resistance, fear, and dread I'd been holding throughout the ten years since my cousin died of AIDS broke loose like an old crumbly dam. I was transfixed on this little, sick, weak, disabled, big-hearted, imaginative, loving, creative, service-oriented boy. I was so emotionally overwhelmed by my desire to be with those in the midst of illness and death that I finally surrendered to it. Out came the flood of tears and the primal wailing sounds that had been held back by a decade of professional obscuring techniques.

I didn't know it at the time, but Mattie was the manifestation of what the Catholic priest Henri Nouwen called "the wounded healer." He was a modern-day manifestation of the bodhisattva Vimalakirti—the ideal lay practitioner in the Mahayana Buddhist tradition. Although I thought my afternoon treat meant doing nothing, I felt compelled to call hospice organizations that very afternoon to see how I could become a volunteer. I give Oprah Winfrey and Mattie Stepanek, now deceased, credit for breaking down my defenses to the reality of living with dying, which revealed to me joy as well as deep sorrow and grief.

A year later, I became a hospice volunteer with Zen Hospice Project (now Zen Caregiver Project). I knew next to nothing about Buddhism when I applied and was not even seeking Buddhist service, but I had the sense that this organization could help me get training in becoming someone who could abide with another, any other, during their last days. Forty hours a week, I was focused on financial services, and five hours a week, I was engaged in hospice volunteer work. Slowly, as the weeks passed, during the work week I would notice my mind lost in daydreams of returning to Laguna Honda Hospital, where Zen Hospice Project had one of its two locations. Those daydreams became more intense, turning into visualizations in which I imagined myself there visiting people I had seen the previous week and not being in the backroom of a mutual fund company. The visualizations began to sap my sense of purpose in my career. I lost interest in sales, service management, and the financial services industry itself because that work was not meeting the overarching need I had to get a grip on the fullness of what it means to be human.

Eventually, I decided to quit my job so as to learn more about Buddhism and spiritual care. I pursued my learning at Sati Center for Buddhist Studies, Holy Names University, and Columbia Theological Seminary, earning a master's and a doctorate degree along the way. I also engaged in supervised residencies in chaplaincy and pastoral counseling. Now, some thirty years after visiting my cousin and twenty years after first becoming involved in hospice, I've had the honor of being with people through all types of life transitions, learning experiences, and crises—the whole range of living and dying. And I am confident in my ability to be with myself and others, no matter what comes our way.

Looking back on how I went from being someone who was unsure she could even attend a funeral to someone whose life is dedicated to witnessing and supporting others, including in the dying process, I am led to the question: How did I work through the fear and uncertainty that burdened me from childhood and well into my adulthood? I didn't work through it alone. I had spiritual friends helping me before I even knew what a spiritual friend was. The term "spiritual friend" is a translation of *kalyana mitta*, from Buddhist Pali, though the role of the spiritual friend is present in all major religious traditions. In this book, I take the concept of spiritual friendship a step further, to the topic and practice of spiritual *kinship*—learning to informally adopt each other, including even those we don't know or with whom we disagree, as siblings, cousins, and so forth. We adopt each other as fellow children of the cosmos. It is common in the black community to introduce really good family friends as "This is my play sister," "That's my play cousin," and so on. I invite all of us to adopt an African sense of belonging, or *ubuntu*, which means, "I am who I am because you are who you are." Rev. Dr. King put it this way in his Oberlin College commencement address in 1965: "I can never be what I ought to be until you are what you ought to be. You can never be what you ought to be until I am what I ought to be. . . . This is the interrelated structure of reality."[3] The idea of becoming spiritual kin is one we'll return to throughout this book, looking at it from individual, communal, and societal perspectives.

Among the spiritual kin who have helped me are then-Zen Hospice Project executive director Frank Ostaseski; volunteer coordinator Eric Poché; my shift mates Fred Malouf and Adam Winkler; Dr. Morgan the pediatrician; the many hospice residents who lived with joy and dread, peace and agitation, and died being cared for; the nurses, and one in particular who laughed at me as I cried carrying a bucket of a patient's particularly pungent feces to the bathroom; the practitioners of the Community of Mindful Living in the San Francisco East Bay Area. There are many more than I have room to mention here, but I'll mention the dharma teacher Lyn Fine for her leadership and Caleb Cushing for his hospitality—who invited me into their sanghas as I studied the teachings of Thich Nhat Hanh; and those practitioners with whom I shared my first meditation retreat, which took place at Spirit Rock Meditation Center, including the dharma teacher Gil Fronsdal.

It was at Spirit Rock, for perhaps the first time since my father died, that I recalled the sound of his voice and saw an image of the movement of his mouth speaking to me. It was in that sitting that I learned, viscerally, that my father was always with me, and I learned again that I could not hold on to him—not the sound of his voice or the image of his mouth.

Flowers and Fingers on the Garland of Our Mutuality

I have shared my story of learning to be with people who are dying—but this is not a book about conventional hospice care. Or I should say, clinical caring for the dying is a model type of situation because of the depth of presence it requires, but it is only one of many types of situations that I will address in this book. This is because my aim is to broaden our understanding of caregiving to include our communal life and our national life. Our collective salvation, from brutality to mutuality, will only happen if we think systemically and structurally. I can only meet with several people a week in my pastoral counseling practice, and large-scale change won't happen this way. So, in this book, I offer a template for thinking and acting as a caregiver or spiritual kin not only toward those in your personal life but also toward the entire network of our mutuality. I'm contending that we can be caregivers to our community, spiritual kinspersons to our society. Although you may at times be surprised that I am extending the concept and practice of professional spiritual care in hospice to lay spiritual care as civility in communal and national contexts, I encourage you to remember that we need to "think big or go home" if we are going to make it together through the challenges we face, environmental and otherwise. If you find yourself outside your comfort zone, see if you can approach that as a chance for growth. And I hope this book will assist you in knowing your place in our network and remind you of your innate goodness. Remember, your thoughts and actions reverberate with the system.

Let's pause for a moment to consider the word "network," as it is a central word and metaphor in this book, and I want to clarify the way I use it. A network can refer to something technical, like the Internet or one's cell phone coverage, or it can refer more colloquially to the connections between a group of people. Networking skills are highly prized in our culture, and I have benefited from learning about how to network. For our contemplative purposes in this book, however, I am interested in a kind of networking done not in order to get what we want but in order to enhance the well-being of individuals and the collective as a whole. Maybe we can call this kind of networking "wholeworking"—connecting with others not simply to achieve success in a career, for example, but to affirm our mutuality. Wholeworking, then, is meeting people to improve the inner workings of ourselves within the network and thus the inner workings of the network itself. It is promoting wholeness through the way we mirror one another—shining a bit more brightly from our place in Indra's Net. Reflecting each other like jewels is not a psychedelic head trip but an alternative way of understanding ourselves through a mystical anthropology—understanding our humanness by transcending all categorization within the web of life.

This is what I understand Dr. King to mean in his phrase "the inescapable network of our mutuality." This is the world of Indra's Net, which I interchangeably call the Net and the Network. Indra's Net is the intricate web of our original and innate mutuality, affirmed at the moment of our birth by those responsible for helping us breathe the first post-womb breath. The Net holds all of our rites of passage in its garment of destiny—that's what Rev. Dr. Martin Luther King Jr. called it—and it exists within every energized atom.

In addition to the Network, there is another metaphor I will use throughout this book to help vivify our situation and our task. It came to me as I considered two iconic Buddhist images. One image, that of a beautiful flower garland worn around one's neck, comes from the Flower Ornament Scripture—the same Buddhist text that elaborates the teaching of Indra's Net. The other image—also a garland, but one hung with severed fingers—comes from the Angulimala or Bloody Finger Garland Scripture, part of the Pali canon of Buddhist texts. We will consider Angulimala's story in chapter 4, but in short, a flower garland represents our basic goodness—our truest nature—while a garland made of bloody fingers represents our destructive tendencies.

Our values and ethical obligations are labile—they are malleable, subject to influence, and therefore subject to attempted exploitation. As a human being, I am a sentient being continually in the process of becoming human. My humanness is not fixed at the outset but is always developing within the flux of my experience. And I believe that the most important choice I make, over and over again within that flux, is whether or not to shape my humanness in the direction of civility, even in the midst of violent threats.

I've heard people critique the concept of civility, saying in essence that clinging fast to civility obscures authentic expression of our feelings under the cover of politeness. Having lived in Minnesota long enough to experience "Minnesota Nice" (a passive-aggressive way of dealing with conflict), by "civility" I don't mean being nice; I mean a complex and dynamic posture toward myself and others informed by a spiritual and ethical sensibility and responsibility. (I find Buddhism's teachings on the Noble Eightfold Path particularly helpful in this regard, and we'll explore those teachings in depth in chapter 2.) This complex and dynamic posture involves a compound of aspirations. It involves trying to accept the truth, even if I don't like it; paying attention to why I do what I do; and, if I find my intentions are harmful, redirecting my energy toward beneficial outcomes for all. It involves paying close attention to the words coming out of my mouth, as well as the tone with which they are said, and noticing their impact on others. It also involves having discipline about my bodily actions so I am not inflicting physical harm and also having discipline as a consumer so as to refrain, as much as possible, from fueling large- and small-scale economies that produce suffering. Last, it involves redirecting my attention to where it needs to be, toward others, with as little judgment as possible, because of the ripple effects throughout the Net. Cultivating a meditation practice supports this civility-oriented posture. All of these aspirations affect the basic choice between civility and brutality.

You have that same challenge and choice. My hope is that the spiritual practices in this book will be a support in that effort. Returning to the garland metaphor, I can say that our invisible garlands may be comprised mostly of flowers or bloody fingers. Throughout life, we are exchanging flowers for fingers and fingers for flowers. My wish is that when we go through the rites of passage out of this life, we leave with more flowers on our garland than fingers. How do you want to go out?

AFFIRMATION
I am a jewel in Indra's Net

Our lives depend on countless things, people, and other beings. Countless things, people, and other beings depend on us. This cosmic interconnection meets at countless points within the net of life. Each point has a jewel-like luminous and reflecting quality. I am a jewel in Indra's Net.

CONTEMPLATION

Five Commitments as You Read This Book

In the interest of your awakening and our collective survival, before you continue reading, please make five commitments as you read this book:

1. Refrain from intentionally killing a sentient being. This book may appeal to your intellect, but your body's impulses are very strong, so try to practice bodily discipline.

2. Refrain from intentionally taking what has not been freely given to you. Being on the path to harming others and consequently losing your freedom will undermine the efforts you are making to learn how to stay out of harm's way.

3. Try to avoid overwhelming your senses with constant gratification so you can feel deep relaxation without grasping and clinging.

4. Refrain from intentionally hurting others with your speech. This book is about making good friends, not making archenemies, so try kind speech first.

5. Refrain from becoming intoxicated, at least while you're reading this book, and experiment with checking in rather than checking out.

If you can commit to these precepts as you read this book, notice how it feels in your mind and body to practice discipline over yourself. This is the path of harmlessness and blamelessness. It feels good and is good to be on this path, so please try to stay on it; otherwise, this book will be more complicated than it is intended to be.

In the end, becoming a spiritual kinsperson—taking up one's place in the Network, exchanging bloody fingers for fragrant flowers—means facing the temptations of toxic homeostasis and intentionally working through the obstacles of partisanship, demonization, and delusion toward the belief and trust in interdependence. This kind of work will remain quite limited if we are unable or unwilling to look at our own and others' suffering. In my private practice in pastoral counseling, I've learned that much of how we suffer has to do with failed relationships, having a sense of self so unworthy that we question our right or ability to sustain healthy relationships, and a larger sense of loss of faith in humanity. When we feel alienated from the network of our mutuality, we effectuate brutality instead. In our suffering, we feel victimized and unable to regain or revitalize a sense of belonging and recognition.

And so, in this book, we will explore different kinds of suffering, especially something I call "mobbery." We will see that expanding our capacity to see and be with suffering is a necessary step in learning how to shift from being self-absorbed to being concerned about others. This process also involves learning how to cultivate compassion, use your imagination to feel yourself as part of the network of our mutuality, and reconcile with others to rebuild a sense of self that is connected and in community. We will explore together how to diminish the defensiveness that deludes and cognitively separates us from ourselves and others, how to lessen the aggression that blinds us to who we and others are, and how to promote empathy that validates our recognition of ourselves and others.

One of our main guides in this book will be ancient wisdom from religious or spiritual traditions. I draw from Buddhism, Taoism, African-inspired wisdom traditions, Christianity, Judaism, Islam, and other traditional sources of insight. You will find, however, that I give myself license to interpret these wisdom teachings to fit our times. Indeed, I have been criticized for taking liberties with Buddhist teachings. The critiques are valid from the standpoint that I am not holding only to the traditional teachings. I am not holding to the traditional teachings exclusively because the traditional teachings, as I understand them, are largely about the transformation of individual suffering. To the extent they apply socially, it is through the belief that when one has transcended one's own suffering, that will impact those in one's life. I believe that to be true to a degree, but when that enlightened individual lives in the midst of mobbery, they are also prone to mob influence. We need more than a traditional reading of our ancient wisdom texts to meet the tension between true freedom and the voracious appetite for authoritarianism.

Though I claim cosmic belonging as the natural state of myself and others and am optimistic about our potential, I am still a heartbroken person. I am not permanently debilitated by heartbreak—I would not be able to write this if so—but I am heartbroken in the sense of witnessing what may well be the downfall of humanity. What used to be a senseless murder here or there has become a senseless *mass* murder here and there, and with such frequency that it is no longer shocking. The easy access to and regular use of rapid-fire machine guns by civilians, including men-children, to murder groups of complete strangers, including schoolchildren, is a cultural sickness in need of healing. It is a sad irony that one of the nation's top healers, television show host Dr. Oz, shows himself locking and loading a machine gun in his political campaign advertisement. And there are so many other reasons for heartbreak: polluted drinking water running from taps designed to deliver potable water, sophisticated buildings crumbling and killing hundreds, violent storms destroying communities, grand lakes drying up before our eyes, and fires too many to count. And all of this against the backdrop of the unskillful ways we express our helplessness—it often leaves me speechless, shaking my head from side to side in not-knowing. Yet, I take heart in the experience of heartbreak, because otherwise I would be living in abject ignorance or sociopathy, and neither one seems like an appealing option.

There is a looming question on my optimistic mind and broken heart that prompts me to write this book: "Can Buddhist practices, whether one is a Buddhist or not, combined with ancient wisdom from various religious, spiritual, and ethical traditions, help us survive each other's brutality?" My chaplain's plea is, "Will you journey with me to find the answer? Please?"

Let us begin this journey throughout the Net with some words from "Lift Every Voice and Sing" by J. Rosamond Johnson and James Weldon Johnson:

We have come over a way that with tears has been watered,
We have come, treading our path through the blood of the
    slaughtered,
Out from the gloomy past,
Till now we stand at last
Where the white gleam of our bright star is cast.[4]

AFFIRMATION
I am worthy of self-compassion

We live in a world where acts of aggression and violence are considered entertaining. Our world is full of countless representations of violence, and we pay for it in every conceivable way—through the coarsening of our hearts, with our hard-earned money, and even with our own lives. We've consumed so much violence and been so affected by the repercussions of violence that we may not even know there are nonviolent alternatives. Violence, however, does not permanently eliminate our capacity for nurturance—one of the first gifts of life. You can return to the experience of original nurturance through self-compassion. Just as true as on the day you were born, you are worthy of self-nurturance. I am worthy of self-compassion.

The Suffering of Mobbery

As I write these words in 2022, there has been a deep stirring in human life over the past several years. This deep stirring is of an existential nature. For example, our environment has become more deadly, and it seems as if we are collectively unwilling or unable to change it. Some call this global warming, others call it climate change, others say there is no change, and still others say these changes are predestined by God to end the evils of human existence, like in the story of Sodom and Gomorrah. In any case, we know landscapes have been altered by heat and storms, property has been destroyed, lives and livestock have been lost, and farms throughout the world have been parched. Changes to the climate and to the viability of regional lifeways are causing people to trek hundreds of miles by foot to enter other countries for food and water without going through legal immigration channels, and such migrations are expected to grow enormously in coming decades. In some countries, there has been a rise in authoritarianism, even in countries once celebrated as remarkable beacons of democracy. Consequently, fellow citizens are turning against one another, desiring more bloody fingers on their garland. When this antagonistic *turning against* starts being enacted not just by one person or small fringe groups but by huge swaths of people, something quite dangerous is happening. I'm coining the term "mobbery" to describe this phenomenon.

Mobbery is a process that centers on anger, energy, and power— it is the aggregation of personal anger into a collective anger that develops a power far beyond that of individuals. Mobbery entails using the energy of anger to find people who are angry about the same things you're angry about, then together harnessing this anger in ways that place blame on others. By taking no responsibility for soothing one's own anger and projecting blame collectively onto groups identified as "other," a new shared reality is created and allowed to harden. The more that angry people gather and strengthen one another, the more their sense of power intensifies. Those identified as others are vilified and attacked, and this is repeated over and over again. This dynamic builds momentum while demonstrating how the power of anger can be exerted on others and how such acts can be interpreted as victories.

It is a core teaching of Buddhism, and other faiths, that one cannot overcome suffering without facing it as it is. For this reason, we will use this opening chapter of the book to look deeply at mobbery—this ominous form of aggression and suffering that seems to be growing in our time. Outlining what mobbery is and how we as individuals choose to participate in it or not will provide a foundation from which we can explore, in subsequent chapters, what it means to live as a caregiver or a spiritual kinsperson—to cultivate the capacity to be with one's own or others' anger, confusion, aggression, or other difficulties without needing to project blame onto others perceived as different. But I am wary of jumping ahead to the solution—first, we need to look closely and deeply at the causes and conditions of mobbery.

Understanding Mobbery

When I think of mobbery, one of the first images that comes to mind, because it was so shocking to the conscience, is of the thousands of people who marched to the US Capitol on January 6, 2021, and attacked it in an attempt to disrupt the confirmation of a new president that year. Although the symbols of discrimination some of them carried, such as Confederate flags and white nationalist paraphernalia, and the violence they committed are deplorable to me, I also believe that many of our fellow citizens may have been surprised by their own "pro-democracy" sentiments turning into an attempted coup that day. On the other hand, many were primed for the attack, having been groomed over several years to think of such violence as normal and warranted. This form of mobbery had been espoused repeatedly in the form of the Hillary Clinton–hate-mongering Republican National Convention of 2016, where many in attendance repeatedly chanted, "Lock her up!" Similarly in the encouragement to physically attack Black Lives Matter activists and receive legal reimbursement from the presidential candidate and the glorifying of violence against investigative journalists, repeatedly calling them the enemy of the people. Many of the so-called rallies in support of Trump were poised for attack, as some of their participants consciously or unconsciously consolidated their energies against those they presumed to be against them.

Taking another example: I have come to accept the public presence in the United States of monuments to enslavers and Confederate military figures because they represent something about the country to which I belong, but of course, I do not honor them—I have the right to ignore them. Yet I must confess that for groups of people to forcibly take down such statues against the wishes of others in their community, bypassing any attempt at civil means, can also be a form of mobbery. Some instances of such actions have been expressions of collective aggression outside the bounds of the legal process. Is it righteous indignation? Do the ends justify the means? Are we engaged in dialogue based in philosophy and ethics? Completely bypassing civil means can diminish the humanity of others; it has been the historical method of self-righteous vigilantes, and it is a method that is being taken up by others, breeding contempt and justification for further self-righteous vigilantism.

I lived in the Netherlands between 1985 and 1987, when the Berlin Wall was still up. I remember arguing with a few German and Dutch peace activists who believed it would be easier to rid the world of nuclear weapons than dismantle the wall. I argued that the wall would come down when enough Germans wanted it down. It came down in 1989, with individuals helping dismantle it, but before those individuals began taking it down, democratically inspired political reforms had taken place in Europe. What democratically inspired actions are we involved in before we begin tearing things down? We should always ask ourselves whether the ends we want to actualize seem likely to justify the means we are considering. As with the January 6 mob, I am certain that many people who have found themselves for the first time tearing down statues or breaking store windows were surprised by the expression of their own aggression. When I worked as a political asylum officer with the Immigration and Naturalization Service (INS), now called US Immigration and Customs Enforcement (ICE), I heard many testimonies, from people of different ethnicities, nationalities, political views, and religions, about the harm human beings inflict on each other. No country is immune from mobbery and large-scale human rights abuses.

I share the above examples not simply to single out particular groups of people but to make the point that mobbery has happened and is happening, and I believe it is likely to become even more prevalent. The fact is, mobbery is as old as the United States—I'm thinking of land grabs, genocide, stealing children from their parents, slavery and other forms of dehumanization, lynching (now a federal hate crime due to the 2022 passage of the Emmett Till Bill), discrimination, a cancel culture that unnecessarily strips someone of their humanity, and so on—we just haven't called it such. Mobbery continues to be an option for people with power and people who want power.

Recent years have shown us so many stories of both mutuality and brutality. There is rising political polarization and racial unrest, increasing climate catastrophes and associated swells of climate refugees, and more opportunities to join protest movements. With all of that being the case, whether you have been part of a mob or subject to a mob before, you might ask yourself, "Is it not likely that I will be faced with choices related to mob behavior in my lifetime?" Seeing how many examples exist around the world and throughout history of people finding themselves acting violently in ways that were never part of their previous self-understanding or professed ethics, I think we each must ask ourselves if we are prepared to face the inevitable invitations to participate in mobbery. I hope that by using this word, "mobbery," along with engaging in mindfulness practices and upholding ethical commitments, we can notice better when we are in its flow and step out of it to avoid preventable harm to ourselves and others.

Here's another example—this one showing both the impulse toward mobbery and a successful response to it. The professional race car driver Darrell "Bubba" Wallace is a black-identified biracial American. In 2020, as the George Floyd–inspired racial reckoning was taking hold, Wallace said on national media that if the National Association for Stock Car Auto Racing (NASCAR), of which he was a racer, wanted its events to be welcoming to all fans, then it would make sense to ban the Confederate flag at their events. NASCAR complied, and both the organization and Wallace weathered the hateful criticism hurled at them. Timing, talent, star-power, ethics, compassion, cultural sensitivity, money, and truth-telling all contributed to this peaceful and civil cultural transformation. Corporations have played a part in our civility project, and we would do well to consider how to partner with them to continue doing so.

I have seen mobbery expressed as the targeting of a group of people (or one person as a representative of that group), blaming them for an offense or crime, and convincing others that one's own group has been hurt by this group. Sometimes, this sense of hurt stems from perceiving one's group as being deprived of a right or entitlement by the other group. Or, going further, that the mere exercise of that same right or entitlement by the other group is taken as a threat to one's own exercise of the same. Such narratives of victimization get repeated over and over again in groups and in media until people become accustomed to vocalizing and embodying their belief in the narrative, sometimes honing it down to a pithy slogan that can be chanted. This chanting is heard by others in the group, fueling more rage. Individuals in the group eventually lose their conscious differentiation regarding their moral and ethical commitments—the felt knowledge that, even as part of a group, they are responsible for themselves as individuals. They have lost their senses and are poised for destruction.

How does this loss of individual agency come about? From a systems perspective, mobbery includes vibrations and resonances with other people that generate a powerful sense of energy. The strong energy is a force to be reckoned with; it can overpower our cognitive functions, causing our cognitive awareness and decision-making processes to become impaired. We become swept up in a collective field that is difficult to escape until the system itself relaxes. What is being lost amid the waves of strong emotion? It's the mature individual adult self that knows wrong from right, harm from healing, and unaccountability from accountability. Whatever the political justification—and I have seen many—the endgame is destruction. Mobbery causes suffering both for the mob members and for the targets of their aggression, and thus it is both an instance of collective suffering and a forward manifestation of collective suffering.

Mobbery can cause lifelong traumas. Mob actions leave deep injuries within people that change them forever. Let's pause for a moment to allow this statement to seep in: a mob action may be momentary, but the wounding may last a lifetime. What message is so important that we must inflict lifelong wounding in order to be heard? What is actually heard after the wounding has been inflicted? I feel confident in saying that the message intended through mobbery is not the message received. The message received is likely to be that the messengers are evil, hateful, violent, careless, narcissistic, selfish, foolish, arrogant, and ultimately, dangerous.

Whenever we resort to mobbery, we have failed. Whatever is achieved through mobbery is stolen because it relies on a partial view of reality—it steals people's access to more mutual and wholesome views and opportunities for collaboration and compromise, and thereby creates the conditions for more mobbery. Instead of casting Indra's Net to include others, mobbery attempts to bunch the Net into artificial and harmful configurations. This kind of mentality will inevitably cause spiritual starvation from the waist up, and those who recognize this will come to ask for a way out of that suffering. In the Buddhist tradition, one who commits to alleviating not only their own suffering but equally that of others is considered to be on the path of the bodhisattva. We can think of a bodhisattva as a kind of profoundly committed pastoral caregiver or spiritual kinsperson—a person who vows to not turn away. There is a similar archetype in Christianity, the Good Samaritan, that we will examine in chapter 4. So, when I think about those who ask for a way out of the suffering of mobbery, sometimes I frame this question for myself like this: How does a bodhisattva begin to live as a bodhisattva? How can I replace the bloody fingers on my garland with fragrant flowers? Deep contemplation is needed to see how we are prone to sacrifice the best parts of ourselves in order to collectively coerce others. Perhaps the first step is simply to believe in our own ability to set ourselves apart from the crowd.

Within mobbery is the desire for relief from suffering. Mobbery holds the belief that if we eliminate the person or group we perceive to be causing our suffering, we will be free from suffering. Employing a version of the Buddha's First Noble Truth, I can say that the way to be free from the kind of suffering that leads to mobbery is the end of the desire that leads to mobbery. It is said that the Buddha asked spiritual seekers to examine the nature of desire and the escape from desire. Mobbery is expressed in what seems to be an unrelenting pursuit of gratification even in the face of contrary truths. Could it be that mobbery exists, in part, because people haven't experienced the deep satisfaction of wholesome desires like the desires for safety, noncoercive connectedness, nurturing relationships, love, and compassion? Would people still be tempted by mobbery if they experienced spiritual pleasures like meditative rapture? In short, meditative rapture is a state where no ego identification or ego gratification take place. Can you imagine that?

CONTEMPLATION
Three Marks of Existence

In Buddhism, a tradition that focuses on understanding the causes, conditions, and relief of suffering, there are three main meditation subjects: impermanence, suffering, and non-self. "Impermanence" is the dynamic of constant change, including the change of coming into and out of existence. "Suffering" is when impermanence is resisted, denied, or defended against. "Non-self" means, among many things, the inability to possess complete control over anything, including one's self-concept. Narcissistic personality disorder (NPD), as it is described in Western psychology, is the most severe case of the self-concept getting out of control, and we will look at NPD in relation to mobbery in chapter 2.

Here's a simple practice. Bring these three meditation objects to mind without meditating:

- Impermanence
- Suffering
- Non-self

Just sit with these truths. Do so now, and do this just for a few minutes a day. What comes up for you? Notice whether you even want to bring to mind the truth of your future death, the truth that craving for the impossible causes you to divert your attention from where it needs to be, and the truth that you are impotent to change these realities. Humbling, isn't it? Stay with it. There is goodness in humility. Notice the desire to assign value. Sit with that feeling. Notice the energy arising in your body. Where is it? Is there a part of you that wants to scream in your ordinariness? If so, who do you want to scream at? What part of you feels most threatened as you sit in the reality of your demise? What weapons do you imagine reaching for to protect what cannot be protected forever? Does your existential terror blind you to the radiance of others? Notice.

Now bring to mind that we are not all out to get you and you are not out to get all others—not really. In this stillness, contemplating these three meditative subjects, we know we have a choice—work with relinquishing delusion or remain in existential terror. As we work with relinquishing delusion by stilling our bodies, we are on the path of equanimity—the state of being at peace with what used to bring us agitation.

Recognizing the Seeds of Mobbery

Although mobbery can end up looking ferocious and complex, the seeds that lead to us dealing with our desire, fear, and insecurity this way are often quite simple. Perhaps they are easiest to see in children.

During my childhood in Indiana in the 1960s and '70s, my family lived in a small house that my parents bought in a neighborhood still experiencing white flight. The last white couple to live on our block —an older couple whose children were grown—were our next-door neighbors, and they stayed many years before retiring and moving to Florida. My neighborhood was black, but my next-door neighbors were white. The United Methodist church in the next neighborhood was pastored by a white man, and there were still white people attending that church when we started there. It became all black by the time I left thirteen years later. I learned about cross-racial adoptions when a white girl at the all-white school I was bused to in the sixth grade invited me to meet her family. I was expecting to meet more white people, but she introduced me to her parents and all her siblings, including two black children! I learned that a twelve-year-old can be a humanitarian. Middle school was also the first place where I experienced a white classmate's attempt to dehumanize me, saying out loud, "Everyone around this table has something in common except her!" He was scowling and pointing at me. I learned that a twelve-year-old can be a racist. These were important lessons I learned in the sixth grade.

In the seventh grade, I began to learn something else. I noticed a shift in what my girlfriends were talking about—boys! They found boys fascinating and captivating. Their talk was about the thrill of being noticed and the nervousness about bodies being in closer proximity. They talked about fantasies of touching and kissing. I felt none of that. Keeping a longer developmental story short, I was a black girl in Indiana in the 1970s growing up gay and didn't know it. I suspect I only avoided being enrolled into conversion therapy because I was able to pass as straight. I know what it is like to be considered pathological.

My point is, as I assess what suffering is, I take into consideration how people treat others based on what they perceive as different and thus inferior or dangerous. In my childhood, I experienced that individuals who were different from me could treat me with respect, and I also experienced how difference could be tagged as a marker of both individual and collective inferiority—a necessary condition for the appearance of mobbery.

Having had these experiences, I know not everyone is willing to express who they are because the consequences may be dire. I know it also to be true that sometimes we are unwilling to express ourselves because we do not know of or believe in our foundational nature. This nature is non-discriminating, but that does not mean it doesn't notice difference. In fact, this deep nature is genuinely curious about difference and even takes delight in variety and difference. This is also the nature that understands our fundamental similarities and acts on those similarities to help others touch into their basic goodness. Returning to our basic goodness is what we have to do for one another to survive the threat and seduction of mobbery.

———

One Sunday morning when I was attending church as a teenager, I heard a bone-chilling scream that came from outside the church walls. It penetrated the stained glass on the side of the building. Due to the high pitch of the scream—in the soprano range—it sounded like it came from a woman. Worship was in session, but I made the decision to rise. We would stand together as part of the United Methodist liturgy when we sang hymns or recited the Nicene Creed, but this time I stood alone because I was impacted by the vibration of horror in that Sunday morning screech. As I began to lift myself off the pew, my aunt, sitting next to me, pulled on my dress hem. I bent down, and she whispered to me that I should sit down, adding, "You don't know who's out there." I said that someone was in distress and that I'd be right back, or something like that.

I left the pew and walked out of the sanctuary into the vestibule and then outside. I walked around the small church building. I didn't see any activity or any injured people. When I returned to the building back through the vestibule, re-entering the sanctuary, I saw that all eyes were on me. The preacher, a lanky older black man with a white Afro, stood in silence. He was hovering over the pulpit, and the choir had not resumed its singing. It seemed like everyone in the pews had turned their bodies toward the sanctuary entrance to see if I would return.

What exactly had taken place? Sounds of horror had entered through the stained glass, and I had risen to the vibration, though doing so was out of synch with the liturgical ritual. I had exited and re-entered the vestibule and the sanctuary. The vestibule was a sacred space of liminality that theoretically prepared us for the weekly rites of passage from secular to spiritual life and back again, and to enter and exit it was a defining religious and spiritual experience for me. So, what did I learn on this occasion of doing so?

I learned very difficult lessons regarding compassionate action. First, you can't depend on everyone to stop what they're doing to attend to someone in distress. Second, even while worshipping, a congregation may place devotion over service, not stopping worship to attend to someone in need. Third, my relatives did not follow me; therefore, their safety was more important to them than mine. Fourth, Christianity, to me, meant caring for those in need, and it doesn't mean that to every Christian. Fifth, I was a risk-taker. These five lessons have guided my consciousness and my steps for decades. When I see people in need, I know not to depend on others to help just because they identify with a particular religious belief, engage in particular religious practices, or even have love in their hearts. Sometimes we have to take the risk of being hurt in order to help, and over time I've learned to be wiser in that endeavor. How can we act compassionately with wisdom? Let's engage in a brief visualization practice.

CONTEMPLATION
The Garland of Flowers and Fingers

Imagine you were just born and were fortunate to be given the breath-food-warmth rite of passage. Let the sensations of breathing be felt deeply; let the feeling of satiation be felt throughout your body. Feel warmth, inside and out. As a newborn, you just received your first flower garland in the form of warm arms, a blanket, or something else to keep you warm. You are held in complete recognition and appreciation, so much so, at times, that the garland of flowers grows into a cradle of flowers. The fragrance pleases you and soothes you in times of distress.

But like all of life, of which you know nothing yet, the flowers begin to die, and you have no ability to do anything about it. Before you are able to anticipate it, because you do not have those cognitive skills as a baby, you are lying in a bed of putridity. Each time you cry for relief, sensing your complete dependency on others and experiencing others becoming a disappointment to you, some of your flowers are replaced by the intensity of your pain and suffering. On some level, you start to blame others for the putridity of your existence, and you imagine inflicting pain on those who are supposed to keep your flower cradle fresh. The bloody fingers on your garland represent the retaliation (first in your unconscious, then in your imagination, and later in your intention and expression) for that pain.

As a chaplain, pastoral counselor, and spiritual director who attends to the suffering of others, I think the suffering that comes from the awareness of all the chaos that has happened and is happening in the world illustrates collective existential angst, what is generally called *dukkha* in Buddhism. If we add this existential angst to the suffering of insignificance and the clinging to entitlement, we have a toxic and readily explosive mix of emotions that can be, has been, and will be weaponized to pit us against each other. This suffering is experienced individually but also collectively, as we are beginning to lose our recognition of each other as related by species, and this loss of recognition is dangerous and even deadly. When we recognize each other as being human, we know there are certain things someone being human needs to survive and thrive. We know how to meet those needs because we know what it takes for our own needs to be met and because we have had previous experiences in meeting the needs of others.

In 2017 in Florida, a black human rights activist approached a hate-mongering white man at a white mob gathering. The black human rights activist asked the white man why he hated black people. The white man said he didn't know. The black activist was moved to hug the white man and the white man allowed it. Why offer a hug when punches had already been thrown by others and even landed on the white man? "I could have hit him, I could have hurt him . . . but something in me said, 'You know what? He just needs love.' . . . It's a step in the right direction. One hug can really change the world. It's really that simple."[1] In 2020, a black supporter of the Black Lives Matter movement in England carried a white anti–Black Lives Matters man out of a mob where the white man had been injured. Why? According to the news report, the black man said, "I want to see equality for everybody. I am a father, a grandfather and I would love to see my young children, my young grandchildren, my nieces, my nephews have a better world than I have lived in. The world I live in has been better than my grandparents and my parents and hopefully we can continue until we have total equality for everyone."[2]

These acts of kindness while people are at their most vulnerable are the manifestations of a radical ahimsa that was not coerced by liberal political correctness. No burdens were placed on these two black men to be other than they truly were—empathetic people showing up for a wounded humanity in the face of threats caused by white existential angst and paranoia. Their responses were compassionate and loving without giving up their dignity. They were not being pressured to be "good black folks" or what some used to call "Uncle Toms" by putting the needs of physically wounded white individuals before their own. They were being selfless—not clinging to political postures related to their racial identifications and without undermining the cause of black liberation. We should look to people like these men for their wisdom, broad perspectives, and Good Samaritan capacities.

Now, it appears we are not so sure that people illegally crossing the border are human beings like we are—seeking safety, shelter, food, and water. We're not sure that those who hold a different political opinion are human beings like we are, with needs just like ours that can only be met by people just like us. Rather than meet the needs of vulnerable people, we are increasingly blaming them for being vulnerable. We fear their vulnerability, and sometimes, we believe their vulnerability is contagious. History tells me that if we continue to let these trends go unreversed, we will have genocide in places we never expected it to happen, or happen again, and people who have never committed a crime in their lives will commit genocidal acts. I believe one of the best ways to prevent genocide is to identify when genocide has happened and identify and interrupt the factors that can lead to the next genocide. The Islamophobia in the United States is in need of vigilant human rights watch, as many Americans supported the attempts to exclude all foreign Muslims from entering the United

States. This reinforces fear of American Muslims, Muslims from other countries who were already in the United States, and people who are perceived to be Muslim, like Sikh men who wear turbans. Were many of the "bloodless" one million–plus deaths in the United States from COVID-19 caused by a genocidal intent in the Executive Office? Did calling COVID-19 "kung flu" result in the significant uptick in anti-Asian violence? Does the claim that many of our elected officials are pedophiles create a condition for mobbery? Did accusing US Supreme Court nominee Ketanji Brown Jackson of being soft on pedophiles bolster the belief that our elected officials are pedophiles? As soon as a critical mass of people believe others are subhuman and not worthy of being alive, we have genocidal factors in need of interruption. We are already being called to choose sharp and potentially blood-letting and blood-shedding sides—perpetrator or victim, eat or be eaten—and what kind of choices are these?

Sister Chan Khong, one of the leading nuns in the Plum Village Buddhist tradition of Thich Nhat Hanh, wrote about such choices in her provocative book *Learning True Love: Practicing Buddhism in a Time of War* (1993). While living in Vietnam during the Vietnam War, Sister Chan Khong, Thich Nhat Hanh, and their fellow Buddhist social work activists had choices to make about attending to the pain and suffering of war victims while also being tempted to take political sides. The main lesson they learned was that in order for them to have less interference in their work, they needed to remain politically neutral. Their political neutrality gave no reason for either the South Vietnamese government or the Viet Cong to accuse them of being on one side or the other—although such accusations sometimes still came. In short, they were not openly for or against a political position but were focused on attending to the pain and suffering and ending the war. This attitude of neutrality is also found in the Plum Village Fourteen Mindfulness Trainings, which I discuss in detail in chapter 8. The First Mindfulness Training reads:

The First Mindfulness Training: *Openness*

Aware of the suffering created by fanaticism and intolerance, we are determined not to be idolatrous about or bound to any doctrine, theory, or ideology, even Buddhist ones. We are committed to seeing the Buddhist teachings as a guiding means that help us learn to look deeply and develop understanding and compassion. They are not doctrines to fight, kill, or die for. We understand that fanaticism in its many forms is the result of perceiving things in a dualistic or discriminative manner. We will train ourselves to look at everything with openness and the insight of interbeing in order to transform dogmatism and violence in ourselves and the world.[3]

Can you imagine adopting this mindfulness training while living wherever you are? In the midst of the rising tides of violence? Are you committed to being aware of the suffering caused by politics and noticing when you might be clinging to dogma? How can we be open so we are not seduced by dualities? This is one way we can embrace neutrality and diminish the lure of mobbery in the face of authoritarianism.

Greed, hate, and delusion are taking hold as natural resources dwindle under climate change, and the resultant forced migrations require better-resourced people to consider sharing. Right now, our technologies make it possible to produce enough to share. When we believe our survival depends on another's deprival, what will we do? What we believe and what we choose to invest in is our way forward.

What will help us move forward in a way that renounces mobbery and embraces differentiation, sanity, and civility?

AFFIRMATION

I let go of my own sense of greatness and surrender with humility to the great wisdom of others

Transforming grandiosity to humility takes practice and time. It may initially feel threatening, but based on the testimonies of some of the greatest people in history, it will be worth it. As you find comfort in humility, your need to act aggressively will subside. Even if no one notices your transformation, you will know that your greatness resides in your ability to transform your aggression, not in being violent. I let go of my own sense of greatness and surrender with humility to the great wisdom of others.

2

Beyond the Golden Rule

Treating Others as They *Need to Be Treated*

In the previous chapter, we looked closely at the phenomenon of mobbery and the suffering that it causes. I described how individuals who succumb to mobbery are relinquishing the responsibility to maintain their own moral autonomy in favor of letting the energy of angry crowds draw out their sense of antagonistic tribalism and violent abandon. Another way to think about mobbery is as the deepening of a collective narcissistic personality disorder NPD, on an individual level, is defined in part as having these elements:

1. A pervasive pattern of grandiosity
2. A need for admiration
3. A lack of empathy

NPD can also include a preoccupation with power, the delusion of being special, exploitativeness, entitlement, envy, or arrogance. This kind of personality, due to its appearance in prominent individuals situated at the top of the executive branch of federal government (and in the two other branches of government), has widened the gateway to believing patriotism is defined by these narcissistic elements. I believe, however, that many of the people who seem to believe in such pseudo-patriotism know in their hearts that it isn't true—that despite their clinging to entitlements, they are not inherently or innately superior to anyone else. In this false sense of self, they often resort to a strict, partial, and historically dubious reading of the Second Amendment to brutally defend their version of patriotism. This distortion of patriotism and uneven weighting of rights is turning us against each other through mobbery. Consequently, we are losing our ability to be compassionate and to unconditionally attend to the suffering of others. But perhaps we are losing it because we don't know we have it in the first place. One of the main tools we have to start to turn this situation around is the capacity to mirror each other empathetically. To "reflect like an untarnished mirror" means diminishing the violent propensities within ourselves so others can feel and see their mirroring potential as well. This mirroring capacity is what Indra's Net is about.

The Austrian-born American psychologist Heinz Kohut (1913–1981) developed a theory and psychotherapeutic method called Self Psychology that can help us live more equanimously with our own narcissistic tendencies and deepen our capacity for mirroring. In summary, Kohut believed that parents who repeatedly fail to show empathy to their baby thereby cause trauma to the child's personality and ego-development processes. The child, even though they were preverbal during the initial period when empathy was lacking, remembers this unempathetic parental attitude and comes to believe they are insufficient and unworthy as a person. This unempathetic parental attitude is sure to be encountered in other people as the child grows older, and their reaction to what appears to be unempathetic can be deeply painful, perhaps felt as depression. This is because it triggers the primal wound regardless of whether the other person is truly unempathetic or is merely perceived that way. One way to protect oneself from this wounding is to engage in behaviors that display the opposite of insufficiency and unworthiness—grandiosity—as a way of defending one's ego against re-experiencing the lack of empathy from others.

Kohut suggested two methods I believe anyone can use to help transform the suffering of narcissism or grandiosity: mirroring and twinning. "Mirroring" is when someone reflects to another that they are worthy of respect. This is done through positively affirming another. Here's an example: Let's say the person caught up in their sense of grandiosity is bragging about something they did. You are irritated because you are conditioned to have an adverse reaction to "braggarts." Mirroring in this situation might look like saying, "I think it is great you have such a talent." Can you see how such a response is a skillful means that decreases the likelihood that the person feels the need to intensify their bragging?

"Twinning" is a way of conveying that you share similar traits, even narcissistic ones, with the person who is immersed in grandiosity. This helps them to not feel weird or isolated in their sense of self. And importantly, this holds true even if it's a person who would never confess their vulnerability to anyone and may not be in touch with it themselves. How might one "twin" in this way? Express that you feel celebratory about their accomplishment because you have also experienced something similar. Mirroring and twinning relational skills help narcissists be in relationship, and those of us using mirroring and twinning (thereby using our own narcissism for good) are also helped by not alienating people who irritate us.

CONTEMPLATION
Attending to Others

Mirroring and twinning may sound like simple practices, and over time, we can come to experience them that way. But when we're new to these ways of being with others, it requires developing qualities of presence that make space for our own anxiety and allow for other-orientation. Here are two practices that help this process:

1. *Cultivate a non-anxious presence*

Mirroring and twinning will not be as effective if your presence carries an undertone—or overtone—of anxiety. If you are generally or situationally anxious, do what you can to work on becoming less anxious. Depending on your particular circumstances and disposition, that may mean attending to healthy relationships, diet, exercise, sleep, meditation or prayer, or therapy. It can also be as simple as noticing when you are not anxious and setting the intention to grow that experience in new directions. If you generally are not anxious, think about the reasons why, and continue doing what you do to live with less anxiety.

To whatever extent you can connect with non-anxious presence, bring that calm to those who are struggling with their suffering. Your non-anxious presence can be a balm and an inspiration for their path to feeling more at ease.

2. *Practice deep perception*

Mirroring and twinning require an accurate perception of the person you are with. The act of deep perceiving (using all the senses available) is one of the most powerfully healing activities we can offer someone in need. We act with deep perception when we:

- Listen deeply for existential angst
- Affirm the emotional experience
- Validate rather than judge
- Encourage and inspire
- Reveal bright eyes and smile because this is what reflecting mirrors, diamonds, and pearls looks like on the face
- Share appreciation
- Share blessings for a fortunate future
- Encourage wisdom teachings
- Warn against the dangers of engaging in violence

We know that creating heaven on earth, metaphorically bowing as we mutually refresh our garlands with fragrant flowers, requires us to create the conditions for living in a world with as little violence and as much access to our basic needs as possible. For some, the reduction of violence begins with opposing abortion or promoting vegetarianism and veganism. It appears the energies of empathy, compassion, loving-kindness, and mutuality are more present when we observe a baby or child who we know is completely dependent on another human being for their survival. What causes us to turn away from the initial interest in life toward its destruction? Once we recognize an older person's ability to survive without help, we leave it to them to fend for themselves. For most of us, without practices like cultivating a non-anxious presence and deep listening, we will be carried along by the cultural inertia of assuming all others can fend for themselves.

Given our proclivity toward competitiveness and brutality, we need to check our perception and ask ourselves, "Just because this person is older and can seem to care for themselves, are they really protected from the brutality that can reduce them at any time to the vulnerability of a child?" Of course, the answer to this reflection is no, but what do we do with that reality, the fact that all of us can be reduced at any moment to the state of vulnerable dependence? What do we do with the psychic aggression that comes forth when we impose the expectation of independence on others? Whether you practice mirroring and twinning or other intentional approaches to being with other people, cultivating non-anxious presence and practicing deep perception are certain to support your effort to have fewer bloody fingers and more fragrant flowers on the garlands of your life.

We will encounter various examples of mirroring and twinning, and other ways to be in relationship amid difficulty, in the subsequent chapters of this book. Several of these chapters look at classic religious parables from different faith traditions through the lens of preventing mobbery and fostering spiritual kinship. Before we go on, however, I want to introduce one additional way of thinking about the transition from what I call the "individual self-template" to a community-minded template. And that is—moving beyond the Golden Rule to the kind of higher order of relational commitment that is necessary to fulfill our potential as spiritual kin.

We've all been taught some version of the Golden Rule: "Do unto others as you would have them do unto you." I don't want to belittle this ethical maxim—it lies at the heart of promoting unconditional civility. It is not based on gender, age, ethnicity, nationality, blood ties, or any of the myriad ways we categorize each other, and I appreciate its recognition of ourselves, our needs, and the shared lived experience between us. Living by the Golden Rule is an invitation to pause before potentially hurting another, but given the rise in mobbery, isn't it time for a rule that promotes even greater relationality? I think we need to transcend the Golden Rule and move toward what I am calling the Platinum Rule: treat others as they need to be treated for their ultimate well-being, not simply as they want to be treated.[1]

Let me say a bit more about the Golden Rule before we look at the Platinum Rule in detail. Abiding by the Golden Rule means we apply our self-template to others because we have been conditioned to believe that if we reflect on our needs first, it will result in a "golden" outcome for another. Sometimes that works just fine, but too often the results are off base because the starting point is self-centered and thus presumptuous. This presumptuousness is commonly expressed, for example, in giving advice to someone who is distressed. Perhaps we believe we'd want advice if we were similarly situated, but have we noticed if the distressed person has asked for advice? When we reflect on our self-template, we often think how uncomfortable the situation would be if we were experiencing the same thing, so we attempt to offer something soothing to others when what we're really doing is soothing our insecurity. Perhaps the other person is not uncomfortable at all, or perhaps they are uncomfortable but in a different way than we imagine. I learned this in my chaplaincy training at Zen Hospice Project (now Zen Caregiving Project). In a role play, someone was distressed and I reached out to touch them. After I touched them, the actor asked me why I did that. I was startled. "Isn't that what you're supposed to do?" This was a question coming from my cultural conditioning. We went on to discuss if what I really experienced called for touch. It did not. My touch interrupted an emotional experience the actor wanted to delve into, and I wasn't ready to go there and didn't trust the actor to be well in that deep dive. Presumptions based on our self-template may be the polite thing to do, but they can also undermine the need for constructive conflict, confrontation, intimacy, curiosity, or creativity.

. Living with the Platinum Rule does not mean throwing out the Golden Rule entirely. Starting with how you want to be treated and treating someone like that is, of course, much better than acting out of suspicion, fear, bias, or cultural assumptions. In some cases, it may be the best starting point. Yet, evolving beyond the Golden Rule template of treating others *only* as we want to be treated opens the door to learning about and respecting difference, and perhaps ultimately gaining cultural competencies we would otherwise never develop.

To decrease the tendency toward mobbery and other forms of harm, we can consider adopting a mantra: "What does this person really need?" Then sometimes actually ask, "What do you really need?" And then consider how that need can be met. We live in a pluralistic society and world, as well as in a postmodern culture with inclinations toward de-classification, de-categorization, de-stigmatization, and so on. In this situation, we are examining more and more the individual, their internal world, and their connections to the external world, and we are doing so with an aversion to clinging to unwanted socially constructed identities. For example, the trans community has been quite successful in introducing a practice of everyone, regardless of identity and expression, self-identifying genders so we reduce the harmful mistakes made in misgendering based on our perceptions. These ways of relating are fueled by empathy, compassion, and respect.

It is time to evolve with intention, so let's move toward the Platinum Rule. I think of the Platinum Rule as having twelve steps or stages. I'll move through them this way in what follows, though these steps or stages are not intended to be rigid or linear—please simply read and make use of them as they resonate with you, taking particular notice of those that cause you discomfort.

Step One: Observe

People are on the move throughout the world due to violence, natural disasters, and the resultant hunger, thirst, and needs for shelter or safety. Forced migrations are causing people, cultures, customs, and beliefs to collide. Some of us feel invaded by strangers and betrayed by our political leaders. Categories of "us" vs. "them," and the "haves" and "have-nots," are compounded by changes that are beyond our control, such as climate change. These changes are disorienting, leading to feelings of insecurity and estrangement in one's "own" land. We have choices before us—resist change or embrace our global kin, wage war or cultivate peace, hoard resources or share generously. Step one of the Platinum Rule is simple, but not easy: observe. Observe your thoughts and emotions about different groups of people. Observe any sense of entitlement, resistance, or fear that arises. And above all, observe how your physical impulses inform your beliefs and vice versa.

Step Two: Be Curious

Though the Golden Rule helps us understand ourselves and others to a degree, it blunts our curiosity about others because what we understand about our "self" forms the beginning and the end of our knowledge of how to treat others. The Golden Rule can be used as a springboard for curiosity. Ask yourself, "Should I treat others as I want to be treated without their permission?" Asking this question reveals a very powerful paradox about the Golden Rule: we should treat others as we treat ourselves *and* we should not treat others as we treat our-selves because we have not sought permission to do so. I think of this as the Curiosity Paradox that forms the bridge between the Golden Rule and the Platinum Rule.

Step Three: Recognize Human Complexity

The Golden Rule helps one recognize one's own human "template," what it means to be one particular human being—yourself. Through that recognition, you will find that you are complicated (comprised of many parts and processes), complex (not reducible to those parts and processes), and discrete while also interconnected. Using the Curiosity Paradox, we learn that we are complicated and complex, that other human beings are complicated and complex, and that Indra's Net is complicated and complex beyond our capacity to comprehend. Through recognizing the human beingness of others, we realize that there are not only similarities but also significant differences between us. Because these differences are sometimes complex, the Golden Rule is severely limited and can cause problems. That is, one's own human template might be experienced as an imposition on another's human template. The Platinum Rule opens us to receiving the other's template as another valid manifestation of being human.

Step Four: Form Intentions toward the Good

The Golden Rule sounds like it is full of good intention—treating others as *we want* to be treated. But there is a difference between intent and impact. What if we have lived a life of self-abuse? Do we want to abuse others? What if we have lived a life in pursuit of having all our wants satisfied? Do we want to satisfy everyone else's wants? Forming intentions toward the good is about being thoughtful before acting, and acting (or refraining from acting) so as to try to bring about positive results *for the other*. But this does not mean doing whatever someone else wants even when we perceive it to be harmful—it means practicing attunement to the well-being of others while living, as near as possible, what Buddhists refer to as a "blameless" life for oneself.

Step Five: Acknowledge Imperfection

The Golden Rule does not require us to check in with others to determine whether treating them as ourselves is a beneficial choice. Living by the Golden Rule is assumed to be beneficial, but our personal human templates are necessarily imperfect, formed as they are by our own desires, wounds, and habitual behaviors. Knowing about our own imperfection, we can momentarily refrain from speaking and acting and allow ourselves to be inspired by the Platinum Rule. Merely having formed intentions toward the good in the past does not mean we have activated those intentions now, in this situation. We can check our intentions through an internal dialogue that surveys the variety of responses we can have to another. We can then remind ourselves that our objective is not to cause harm and choose the behavior or behaviors that we believe will be most beneficial to the other. Bringing observation and curiosity to bear, if we cannot determine whether our behavior or refraining from behavior had a beneficial impact, we can ask others about the impact we had on them.

Step Six: See Others as Kin

The Golden Rule is usually seen as a way to form connection, but when it skips over meaningful differences, the connection formed may be superficial or misleading. The Platinum Rule asks that we take a leap of faith to believe that somewhere, somehow, we are *deeply* related even in the midst of our differing appearances or beliefs. For example, if the white segregationist Strom Thurmond, the late US senator from South Carolina, could possibly be related to Rev. Al Sharpton, an

African American Christian pastor and civil rights activist, then you too are certainly related to others who don't look like you, think like you, act like you—or want exactly what you want. Seeing each other as kin on an instinctual level means I recognize you as a relative and thereby hold the potential to care about you. The Platinum Rule does away with a competitive notion like "blood is thicker than water" and replaces it with an ethic of communal interconnection: "There is water in blood."

Step Seven: Transform Your Narcissism

The Golden Rule has served civilization well in helping us connect to one another through the cultivation of empathy. But because we are imperfect beings using ourselves as templates for how to treat other imperfect human beings, we run the risk of narcissism—believing that who we are, what we believe, and how we act is the superior way to be and live. Compounding this deluded self-aggrandizement is the rise in the use of social media. Sharing information about ourselves to large groups of people for their approval has unfortunately become the greatest source of validation for many of us. The Platinum Rule requires us to work harder and make a greater investment in self-transformation in order to bring about good. We mirror and twin others, even and especially those we don't initially understand, and we work to allow others to mirror and twin because doing so supports our growth in relational skills.

Step Eight: Cultivate Selflessness

As the Platinum Rule begins to take hold in our lives, as self-reflection deepens, and as narcissistic tendencies start to abate, there is a greater likelihood for compassion, lovingkindness, empathy, and interpathy to flower. "Interpathy" is a word coined by pastoral theologian David

W. Augsburger that means "being able to enter a second culture cognitively and affectively, to perceive and conceptualize the internal coherence that links the elements of the culture into a dynamic interrelatedness, and to respect that culture (with its strengths and weaknesses) as equally valid as one's own."[2] In addition to curiosity, empathy, and interpathy come generosity and a joy that arises from this new orientation toward others. These kinds of felt energy counter depression, meaninglessness, isolation, alienation, and purpose-lessness. Selflessness increases our capacity to be present for another's needs.

I was unexpectedly called into interpathic space while putting the finishing touches on this book. I sent the manuscript to a Hindu chaplain who shared via email that my many uses of the word "caste," coupled with the fact that I'm grounding my writing in Buddhism (seen by some as superior to Hinduism), might fuel Hinduphobia. Shocked by my own cultural insensitivity and fearful that my love for the Bhagavad Gita might actually inspire loathing of Hindu people, I called the chaplain right away to understand their perspec-tive. I listened and I understood. I recalled when I was in an interreli-gious immersion group with people who refused to go into a Hindu temple (on religious grounds) but entered the houses of worship and practice for every other religious tradition we visited. I remembered my Hindu roommate in law school who gave me her Kali statue that remains on my altar to this day. I brought to mind my Hindu neighbor who burns incense outside his door in the morning—a ritual that brings me pause, appreciation, and joy. I remembered his children, whom I've adopted as my play grandchildren. I recalled my history with the word "caste" and remembered that I was not initially taught about the British colonial form of classifying people that was imposed on India. The chaplain was correct when she pointed out that

Hindus are scapegoated for the modern caste system and that they are unfairly punished for it. This is wrong. I do not want to perpetuate Hinduphobia. I chose to edit my manuscript in the "eleventh hour" in the interest of promoting truth, complexity, respect, and spiritual kinship. This is an example of how I've practiced interpathy.

Step Nine: Speak the Truth for the Benefit of Others

Assaults on the media, the use of the label "fake news" even for real investigative reporting, attacks on scientific findings particular to climate change and infectious diseases as "hoaxes"—these and related phenomena have diminished one of the greatest ethical values for the evolution of a civilized humanity: truth. In a lie-based cultural context, the Golden Rule can manifest in the sentiment, "I don't want to hear the truth, so I won't tell you the truth." The Platinum Rule, in helping transform narcissism, paradoxically helps us strengthen our egos enough to handle hearing truths that might be difficult to bear, even those that concern ourselves. It also helps us to tell difficult truths to others while maintaining the intention to bring about beneficial outcomes.

Step Ten: Practice Appreciative Listening

Most people want to be heard when they speak, but many people do not say what they really want to say about their experiences of vulnerability. This is usually for fear of being shamed, ridiculed, rejected, or exploited. The inability to speak one's truth means we live in inauthentic expression, leading oftentimes to meaningless chatter to fill the gaps of the uncomfortable silence between strangers. The Platinum Rule helps us form the intention to listen to others with the ears of appreciation—appreciating the fact that, no matter what is initially said, we are taking in the miracle of a unique human being.

This person exists and has an embodied combination of experiences, stories, perspectives, concerns, and obligations. Their life is full of complicatedness and complexity. Appreciative listening can lead to the kind of awe that increases curiosity; it is a type of listening that invites others out of their fear of being shamed or exploited and into flourishing, revelation, insight, genuine friendship, and solidarity.

Step Eleven: Witness the Expansive Potential in Others

The Golden Rule does not require us to understand how we can live up to our greatest human potential. What if I want to be treated in a way that never challenges me, and so I never challenge you? Consequently, when we live by the Golden Rule, we limit ourselves to who we presently are. A developmental and spiritual interpretation of the Platinum Rule suggests that we treat others as they need to be treated for their ultimate well-being. It challenges us to develop our faith in the capacity of humans to change and evolve, and it invites us to see ourselves and others beyond our superficial and temporary presentations. Enacting the Platinum Rule allows us to express surprise and awe when someone attempts to push past their self-limits. Witnessing the expansive potential in others inspires goodness through the mirroring of wholesome pleasure—the feeling of ease that comes in the presence of the good and the vanishing of negativity. When we witness in this way, shame, ridicule, rejection, and exploitation may be diminished, giving way to a sense of pride, self-acceptance, and healthy boundaries.

Step Twelve: Rest-Reflect-Recharge-Return

The Platinum Rule orients us toward the ultimate well-being of others even when we don't treat ourselves that way—that is, when we don't remain curious about our own potential and well-being, instead opting for habitual desires and familiar behaviors. In order to protect ourselves against the burnout that can come when we don't apply the Platinum Rule to ourselves, we need to commit to the curative cycle of rest-reflect-recharge-return (the Four Rs). Without such restorative cycles, the Platinum Rule, just like any other rule for relating, can be utilized in unwise ways. The Four Rs that constitute the twelfth step could, paradoxically and interrelatedly, be the first step. Imagine disregarding steps one through eleven and just living the Four Rs to begin with. To live regularly into the twelfth step prepares us for all the other steps, restores us between steps, and helps us experience all these steps as being in service of the cultivation of a non-anxious presence when we are with others.

A F F I R M A T I O N

*I commit to the ongoing journey of being
mirrored and twinned as I learn to do the same*

Some things seem to come in an instant, and we have been conditioned to expect that our desires will be met immediately. But the path of wisdom requires taking countless steps and encountering many wise ones along the way. Trust that as you learn to mirror and twin and as you allow yourself to be vulnerable as others mirror and twin you, you will do your best to lead others and let others lead you away from mobbery. I commit to the ongoing journey of being mirrored and twinned as I learn to do the same.

3

The Four Noble Truths as a
Path of Mutuality and Relationality

Mobbery, as we have seen, is the rising social phenomenon that consists of a compounding of our narcissistic suffering for the purposes of taking from others that which has not been freely given. It is a cultural expression of unethical behavior that was considered fringe and has become increasingly mainstream. It undermines civility in many ways, one being that it invites people into a warped cost-benefit analysis—that is, "If I rob someone, it will be easier to identify me, but if I join a mob to rob, I may never be identified."

Mobbery is disconcerting to those who accept the truth that our interconnection, be it mutual or brutal, remains inescapable. In short, even if we resort to mobbery and brutality, we will still live with each other because our interconnection is woven into the fabric of reality. Indra's Net brooks no exceptions. No matter how much we label one another, create boundaries, build walls, reify nations, pass legislation, reinforce classes and castes, construct racial and ethnic categories, privilege ourselves over other species, and so on, we will still live in an inescapable network. Even if we move to another country, we will live in an inescapable global network. If we ever live on other planets, we will still live in an inescapable cosmic network. Given this reality, why not work toward a network of which we are already a part, that promotes the reality of our mutuality over the choices we make to be brutal?

I believe that Buddhist thought can contribute to helping us fulfill our mutuality, and in this chapter, we will approach one of the religion's most traditional teachings—the Four Noble Truths, the third of which unfolds into the Noble Eightfold Path—from the perspective of understanding and addressing mobbery. The Four Noble Truths and Noble Eightfold Path were first conceived out of one person's enlightenment experience from the profound ignorance of their existential situation. In Buddhism, it is said that the profound ignorance from which the Buddha became enlightened consisted of not understanding the nature of suffering. This view, and the teachings that unfold from it, can be reimagined, expanded, and applied to our collective relief from suffering. The way to transform this kind of ignorance is to understand suffering and its end by cultivating and possessing the eight folds of the path:

1. Right View
2. Right Intention
3. Right Speech
4. Right Action
5. Right Livelihood
6. Right Effort
7. Right Mindfulness
8. Right Concentration

The kind of suffering addressed in this book, the ignorance of our inescapable interconnectedness and the brutality that are consequences of this ignorance, is not just about our individual ignorance, as classical Buddhism taught, but about our collective ignorance and lack of will, power, or influence to alleviate our collective suffering. Collectively, we are profoundly ignorant of our interconnection and anxious about our interdependence. We can grow in knowledge and take delight in our true nature if we make relationality our top priority.

Adopting the Perspective of Relationality

Let's look at the traditional Four Noble Truths and the Eightfold Path from the perspective of relationality:

1. We suffer from impaired relationality.
2. There are causes for our relational impairment.
3. Relational impairment can be healed.
4. Relational impairment can be healed through the Noble Eightfold Path.

The fourth truth includes cultivating and possessing the right

1. View of ourselves in relationships;
2. Intention to form healthy relationships;
3. Speech that supports relating to one another in ways that minimize harm;
4. Actions that invite one another into healthy relationships;
5. Livelihood that promotes healthy relationships;
6. Effort that promotes mutuality in relationships;

7. Mindfulness that promotes healthy relationships;
8. Concentration that reveals our individual and collective true nature, which informs us about true mutuality in relationships with one another.

With a shift in intention away from privileging only our own awakening toward awakening in relationship, the traditional Noble Four-Eight framework becomes the truth and path toward a noble mutuality and relationality. I believe this shift in perspective offers societal healing, support for cultivating civility, and a prophylactic for undermining the effects of an increasingly violent culture. Is this reimagining of the traditional Noble Four-Eight framework troublesome?

I look at the traditional Noble Eightfold Path as a form of cognitive behavioral psychology for reducing the dysthymic (chronically irritable) or depressive impacts of our cognitive tendencies, which lead us to focus on the negative, catastrophize, or become paranoid— all of which cause us to vilify and discriminate against each other. In terms of personality disorders, Buddhist psychology, in which I place the Noble Eightfold Path, is most concerned with the suffering of narcissism—a cause and condition of mobbery. Can practicing the Noble Eightfold Path of Mutuality and Relationality help prevent our participation in mobbery? I think it holds promise.

The Four Noble Truths of Relationality and Mutuality and the Noble Eightfold Path of Mutuality and Relationality support the notion that mobbery is caused by ignorance of oneself and others, greed for constantly having things our way, and hatred because the binding energy between people in a mob is anger tilted toward violence. Suffering is exacerbated when ignorance is exploited. Case in point: there is nothing in the US Constitution that empowers the vice president to overturn an election, yet a US president publicly said such, people believed it, and the loyal but unempowered vice president became a target of murderous intent by people in his own party. When something like a virus is invisible, ignorance of its existence is easy to exploit. We cannot see the viruses that cause a cold and the flu, and we cannot see noxious gases like carbon monoxide or the chemicals on the chemistry chart of elements, but we know they exist. The exploitation of another's ignorance can be so powerful that it can lead people to deny their own lived experience, as many people who were dying of COVID-19 did while in the hospital being treated by medical professionals who diagnosed it. Mobbery, in the form of threats of political ostracization, fueled COVID-19 denial as an act of patriotism.

Mobbery has been used to impose the belief that COVID-19 is a conspiracy, that Black Lives Matter activists are "disgusting," that white skin is imbued with a magical substance, that stealing from stores during a riot is justice, that scaling the walls of the US Capitol is "political discourse," and that forcibly toppling statues of Confederate war heroes is an end that justifies the means. The justifications for mobbery, whatever the end, create a slippery slope downward into an incivility that causes fear and distrust of each other. Mobbery causes suffering for its members and the targets of their aggression. Thus, it is collective suffering and the manifestation of collective suffering. Mobbery is aggregated dukkha (a Buddhist word for suffering), and a maladaptive form of conflict resolution because it proliferates conflict. But there are alternatives, one being the proper use of democratic systems, which requires patience, wisdom, and the ability to abide with deferred gratification.

Uplifting the truth and wisdom of our mutuality and innate rationality depends on each of us embracing the true nature of our material selves, and doing so is supported by our commitment to see ourselves just as we are, with Right View of Mutuality and Relationality.

Right View of Mutuality and Relationality

Right View of Mutuality and Relationality is not just having a correct opinion; it is an aspect of the Noble Eightfold Path toward the cessation of suffering. This includes understanding what is wholesome and nutritious, as well as contemplating the Four Noble Truths. It also includes meditating on the facts of birth, aging, and death; being, clinging, and craving, as well as the emotions that arise from them. It includes experiencing consciousness and its causes and conditions, as well as ignorance and its causes and conditions. Right View of Mutuality and Relationality is a complex dynamic that can never be fully represented in words, but one way to put it is that it means cultivating Buddha perspective. By "Buddha perspective," I mean the mind of awakening and the sight of clear seeing. Right View of Mutuality and Relationality means being inclined to awakening and having one's perspective inclined toward awakening. Awakening to what? To lovingkindness. I like to look to the Metta Sutta (Lovingkindness Sutra), a teaching from the Buddhist Pali canon, for inspiration in this regard. It states:

To reach the state of peace
One skilled in the good
Should be
Capable and upright
Straightforward and easy to speak to,

Gentle and not proud,
Contented and easily supported,
Living lightly and with few duties,
Wise and with sense calmed,
Not arrogant and without greed for supporters,
And should not do the least thing that the wise would criticize.

[One, should reflect:]

"May all be happy and secure;
May all beings be happy at heart.
All living beings, whether weak or strong,
Tall, large, medium, or short,
Tiny or big,
Seen or unseen,
Near or distant,
Born or to be born,
May they all be happy.
Let no one deceive another
Or despise anyone anywhere;
Let no one through anger or aversion
Wish for others to suffer."

As a mother would risk her own life
To protect her child, her only child,
So, toward all beings should one
Cultivate a boundless heart,
With loving-kindness for the whole world should one
Cultivate a boundless heart,
Above, below, and all around

Without obstruction, without hate and without ill-will.
Standing or walking, sitting or lying down,
Whenever one is awake,
May one stay with this recollection.
This is called a sublime abiding, here and now.
One who is virtuous, endowed with vision,
Not taken by views,
And having overcome all greed for sensual pleasure
Will not be reborn again.[1]

We are inclining ourselves to awaken to lovingkindness, and our collective ultimate purpose, to advance civility, depends on it. We are also awakening to wisdom, to interdependence, to the Middle Way of equanimity, to compassion, lovingkindness, sympathetic joy, and non-self. Why? If we don't advance the civility that humans can actively co-construct, we will actively continue on the path of destruction through chaos. Now that we have experienced chaos writ large—climate change, pandemic, devaluing democratic institutions, opioid addictions from medicine ostensibly meant to alleviate pain, mass migrations, an appetite for authoritarianism and mobbery, and so on—we have a lived and shared experience of understanding how collective chaos does not work for us. Do you intend to perpetuate collective chaos or civility?

Right Intention of Mutuality and Relationality

Right Intention of Mutuality and Relationality means cultivating Buddha intention. Before the historical person Siddhartha Gautama became the Buddha, he was curious to know what life was about beyond all the wealthy finery of the powerful warrior caste he was born into and that he was bound to inherit had he stayed in his caste-oriented place.[2] Cultivating the Right Intention of Mutuality and Relationality means being curious about what is true and accepting what is true, even if the truth runs counter to what you believed and even if the truth feels painful. Within Right Intention is also ahimsa, nonviolence. Given that Right View of Mutuality and Relationality includes the elements to counter suffering, Right Intention means not purposefully causing suffering.

Mob members gather to consolidate violent power, like atoms consolidating to form nuclear energy. The energy can be used in different ways, but the energy itself has no intention other than consolidation. Consolidated energy can be directed and redirected. A mob's consolidation of energy is usually not redirected without force. Forming Right Intention of Mutuality and Relationality means avoiding participating in mobs, but that doesn't mean one cannot voice their opinions and views. Is there a way to do that, in the land of First Amendment free speech that acknowledges our mutuality and promotes relationality in the public square marketplace of ideas?

Right Speech of Mutuality and Relationality

Right Speech of Mutuality and Relationality means paying attention to Buddha mind and to those with whom you will speak so that you don't encourage people to think and act violently. The Buddha traveled with many adherents from place to place. I know of no Buddha stories that include the use of force to enter another's territory. I know of no such stories that include the justification of coercive or manipulative speech. Speech used to encourage others to join a mob is Wrong Speech because it incites violence and discriminatory thinking and behaving. It is important to note one's influence. If people hang on to your every word, be extra careful. If it seems no one tends to listen to you, and you want to be heard, pay attention to what you are saying and to what lengths you will go to be heard. Keeping Buddha mind in mind, it may be wise to say as little as possible until you grow into your capacity to offer speech that avoids intentional harm.

Right Action of Mutuality and Relationality

Right Action of Mutuality and Relationality means paying attention to one's behavior so that the behavior has a benevolent impact or helps mitigate harm. As it relates to mobbery, we simply refrain from participating in a mob. When engaged in an angry group that hasn't become a mob yet, we can use the Right Speech of Mutuality and Relationality to discourage anger from intensifying. In this way, Right Action is the same as Right Speech, and Right Action/Right Speech is motivated by Right Intention informed by Right View, all in the service of mutuality and relationality.

Right Livelihood of Mutuality and Relationality

Some mobs form organically as the result of an immediate event that people are responding to and want a quick resolution. Other mobs lay dormant as their representatives advocate and lobby for the latent mob's interests. These representatives and advocates earn their income from the latent mob. In the Noble Eightfold Path of Mutuality and Relationality, the path factor called the Right Livelihood of Mutuality and Relationality is a moral economic imperative to refrain from economically profiting from causing harm. Mob leaders earning their income from the violence perpetrated by mobbery are not living congruently with Right Livelihood of Mutuality and Relationality. Mob members contributing membership dues, for example, to support the violent acts of the organization also are not living congruently with Right Livelihood of Mutuality and Relationality because their membership dues support and fuel the leadership that advocates violence. One of the greatest lessons I learned about the Right Live-lihood of Mutuality and Relationality came not from Buddhism but from experiences I had of racial discrimination, exploitation, and divestment from South Africa.

In 1984, when I was a recent college graduate, I went to Zimbabwe and Zambia with Operation Crossroads Africa, Inc. Zimbabwe and Zambia border South Africa. I was not destined to leave the United States. In fact, I was about to graduate from college with no career plan. During my last year of college, I developed a self-diagnosed sleep disorder. I'd stay up all night, go to class, then sleep deeply during every class. I'd work two jobs, go home and do homework throughout the night, then go to each class and sleep soundly. This continued until one day, a life-changing professor, Dr. Hal Chase, approached my desk while I was sleeping in his black history class. I believe he pounded on my desk. I was startled out of my sleep to see that my classmates' eyes were on me. I was embarrassed. Dr. Chase told me that I was no longer allowed to sleep in his class. I guess I just needed a bit of fear and humiliation to remain awake! At the end of class, he invited me to visit him during his office hours. Out of guilt or shame or helplessness, I did. When we spoke, Dr. Chase asked me what I planned to do after college. I told him that I had been accepted into the master's program in sociology. He thought that continuing my education by earning a master's degree was a bad idea, given that I was sleeping in class. I couldn't argue with that. He diagnosed my sleeping problem as being caused by "over-institutionalization" and recommended a cure—that I postpone the master's program in order to see the world. He introduced me to one of his former students who had visited Sierra Leone. We talked, and within days, the course of my life and interests changed dramatically. I was no longer sleeping in class, and a few months later, there I was—a black American in Zimbabwe.

In 1984, as a black woman from the United States, I could not enter South Africa because South Africa was a racially segregated and racially caste-oriented apartheid state that could legally prohibit foreign black people from entering the country. In short, the white people I traveled with could enter, but I could not.

Black South Africans, indigenous to the lands consolidated under the name South Africa, were considered by European colonizers as aliens in their own lands and thus lesser beings. Considered as greater beings, the colonizers forcibly constructed a society and an economy where white people profited from the labor of black people and exploited and exported the natural resources of the country.

When I returned to Indiana, in shock from having seen worlds and people far away from home, I knew I could not simply return to a lifestyle of ignorance. I had to leave and live abroad. I applied to the Peace Corps, hoping I could return to an African country, but the Peace Corps said they needed volunteers with technical skills for their Africa projects. I had no such skills, but they thought I could probably teach English to Spanish-speaking people, so they suggested I volunteer in two countries in Central America. Before my trip to Zimbabwe, I think I would have taken the opportunity, but my political education in Zimbabwe taught me to be more aware of the United States' geopolitical interests. Given the US president and his administration at the time, I thought it unwise to represent the United States in these countries, but desperate to leave the United States and live in the world outside the political naivete and global ignorance I grew up with, I researched other overseas volunteer organizations, joined Brethren Volunteer Service (BVS), and lived in the Netherlands for two years.

In 1988, through volunteering with BVS again, I was able to volunteer for the Washington Office on Africa, an organization advocating for divestment from South Africa and freedom for black people in the country, and I also began volunteering for the American Civil Liberties Union. By 1990, more than two hundred US companies ended their business dealings with South Africa. It is estimated that the worldwide divestment movement resulted in a loss of $1 billion in investments. Between 1990 and 1993, de jure apartheid ended. Right Livelihood of Mutuality and Relationality means working in ways that are mutually enriching, reverse impoverishment, and are nonexploitative. It may require refraining from investing in agents of harm. How do we determine how we want to bring about change?

Right Effort of Mutuality and Relationality

Right Effort of Mutuality and Relationality is about acknowledging that we have volition (some ability to move) and agency (some freedom to decide how we are going to move), but just because we have volition and agency does not mean that the utilization of these powers will have a positive effect. For example, if you are angry and you want to bring about change, you can join an angry group, and you can use your speech to rile the crowd. Maybe the crowd will follow your lead, and you can see your effort paying off. But from a Buddhist perspective, this is not Right Effort of Mutuality and Relationality because the intention is to harm. In the context of mobbery, Right Effort of Mutuality and Relationality means using our volition and agency to redirect the energy of destruction onto the path of constructiveness. How? It is a risky endeavor. You can leave the crowd, and that will minimally decrease the energy, but before you go, why not invite others to come with you? Divest the crowd of people and energy, perhaps by creating a counterprotest that doesn't involve the expressions of rage but of peaceful dialogue and deep listening. Right Effort, including Right Speech, includes paying attention to the ways we infuse our political rhetoric with paranoid fantasies and catastrophic thinking. For example, just because someone advocates for a form of gun control doesn't mean communists are out to overturn the Second Amendment right to bear arms through pedophiles who run Congress with ties to deep-state actors bent on destroying the United States. Are you able to see through that? We need to notice when our volition and agency are linked to fear, misperceptions, and runaway paranoia. Right Mindfulness of Mutuality and Relationality contributes to our ability to know when we are caught in fear and confusion.

Right Mindfulness of Mutuality and Relationality

Right Mindfulness of Mutuality and Relationality means being aware without judgment about people—our connections to them and their connections to us. When we begin practicing mindfulness, or awareness, it is likely judgments will arise because our minds have been conditioned to think polemically—this or that, black or white, past or present, up or down, good or bad, and so on. Life is way more complex than the binaries we categorize phenomena into. Through mindfulness of thoughts, we practice observing how thoughts come and go, and through mindfulness of the mind, we observe the state of our mind—calm, agitated, disorganized, or whatever the case may be. One of the problems with being caught up in a crowd, rageful mob or otherwise, is that the strong vibrational quality of the crowd physically impacts the body, of which the mind is a part. Such vibrations can quickly overtake our ability to think clearly unless we are well-practiced in mindful awareness so that we can remove our bodies from the collective body of the mob. In order to change our view of ourselves and others from innate enemies to potential allies, a real possibility through Right Mindfulness of Mutuality and Relationality, we will need to understand our innate capacity for kinship.

Right Concentration of Mutuality and Relationality

Right Concentration of Mutuality and Relationality means deep meditation on the nature and experience of our emptiness, or inter-penetration. It means taking the object of our meditation as the reality of our interrelatedness. Meditative concentration on emptiness leads to a noumenal experience—something beyond our senses and thus something beyond anyone's ability to precisely describe. As some might say, "It is what it is." Others may call it "suchness" or "the way."

Part of the practice of integrating these truths and path factors into our consciousness is repeatedly reflecting on Right View, arguably the foundation for all the interrelated path factors, and returning to Right View can be a useful touchstone for our reflection. Again, Right View is complex and even more complex in the context of mutuality and relationality, and contributing to its complexity are the evaluations of what is wholesome.

On Wholesomeness and Its Roots

Wholesomeness is actually a limitless quality that includes non-competitiveness; non-coerciveness; and not desiring to control others' perceptions, reactions, and responses to what they experience. In this sense, it is anti-gaslighting, and its overall effect is to produce what is beneficial. The opposite of wholesomeness is unwholesomeness. Unwholesomeness includes being competitive and manipulative. To compare, we can create two lists that may look like this:

Unwholesome (Bloody Fingers)	Wholesome (Fragrant Flowers)
Killing living beings	Abstention from killing
Taking what is not given	Abstention from taking what isn't given
Misconduct in sensual pleasures	Abstention from misconduct in sensual pleasures
False speech	Abstention from false speech
Malicious speech	Abstention from malicious speech
Harsh speech	Abstention from harsh speech
Gossip	Abstention from gossip
Covetousness	Abstention from covetousness
Ill will	Non-ill will
Wrong View	Right View

The causes or roots of these unwholesome and wholesome states are:

Unwholesome Root	Wholesome Root
Greed	Non-greed
Hate	Non-hate
Delusion	Non-delusion

There's a root underneath these roots, and it is the perpetual quest to find and sustain sensual pleasure—in short, addiction. I am talking about being in the constant state of pursuing experiences that feel good. In this never-ending pursuit of pleasure, we avoid things we have to do that don't feel good, and we also avoid feeling what has to be felt. Many people object to Buddhism on the grounds that it is said to prohibit the happiness found in pleasure—that it is paradoxically nihilistic at its cosmological core—but I believe that to be a reductive misinterpretation of the teachings as a whole. When we reflect on what it means to be part of a network of equals, in mutuality, existing in a matrix of cause and effect because we are nodes in Indra's Net, we can't really deny that what we do impacts others, just as what others do impacts us. The constant pursuit of pleasure and the attempts to maintain that state obscure the existence of others and prevent others from seeing our authentic selves. What others see is a distortion or a reduction of ourselves into a protracted impulse.

The momentary experience of pleasure is not problematic; it is what surrounds and perpetuates that moment that is problematic. These experiences of pleasure, surrounded and followed by unwholesome states of mind and behaviors, can be tested in the context of spiritual community. The spiritual community need not fall into just one religious tradition, but it should be a spiritual community that respects life, supports wholesomeness, teaches people how to refrain from unwholesome thoughts and behaviors, supports the transparency of our authentic selves, and teaches lessons on how to relate to others like and unlike ourselves—without discrimination.

AFFIRMATION
I dedicate the rest of my life to the welfare of others

Recognizing the damage violence causes in our lives, I renounce violence as a means of getting what I want just because I want it. Letting go of self-aggrandizement, I embrace humility and celebrate wisdom and acknowledge that being on the path is liberation. I dedicate the rest of my life to the welfare of others.

4

"Say What?"

Koans as Relational Wholeworking in Stories of Jesus, the Canaanite Woman, and Angulimala

When Yeshua and his Hebrew disciples were traveling in Canaan, they encountered a Canaanite (thus, polytheistic) woman who begged Yeshua to heal her child.* Yeshua's disciples encouraged him to ignore her; the group attempted to bypass her. She kept after Yeshua and, in his annoyance, he told her that they were not there to speak to the Canaanite people but to their own people, the Hebrews. She already knew that, for previously, according to the Bible, the Hebrews had been on a genocidal mission to rid the world of Canaanite people. Yet, she persisted. Yeshua's annoyance turned toward a mind of belittling. He likened her and the Canaanite people to dogs. How did she respond? Her child was sick! The woman's mind was on her child being well and, because Yeshua's reputation preceded him, she believed he could heal her child despite his arrogance and insensitivity. So, she didn't

* In my telling of this parable, I use Jesus's Hebrew name, Yeshua, to help readers feel the kind of cross-ethnic difference that is such an important part of the story.

give up, instead saying to Yeshua that even dogs eat the scraps from their master's table.

Say what? Why would this woman, alone, facing a group of men belittling her, reach for a provocative analogy that seems to affirm their lowly views of her? My take is that she was using a koan—a phrase that seems or is nonsensical and is used to disrupt unnecessary dualistic discursiveness. Koans are used in Zen Buddhism to talk about an exchange between a wise person and their student. Often, the student is trying to answer a question that doesn't need to be answered, according to the teacher, because it takes the student's mind away from what really matters—liberation from unnecessary discursiveness and duality. One of the purposes of using koans is to disrupt discursiveness in such a way that thought processes stop, then return to what is essential (like dwelling in mind) or morally important. In the Zen tradition, such disruptions are used as tools to help students toward awakening. Because dualism can ultimately lead to brutality in its most extreme forms, koans can also be taken as a model for relational and communal wholeworking: taking situations that could turn brutal and instead steering them toward mutuality, which can be an awakening experience in its own right. Here's an example of a classic koan from Zen:

An old, presumably uneducated woman of no pastoral authority encountered a Buddhist scholar named Te-shan Hsan-chien in her tea shop. Entering the shop, he asked for a treat called *mou mou*. "Mou mou" has a double meaning—*culinary refreshment* and *mind freshener*. Te-shan said he had traveled to the area to find people claiming to have awakened without intensely studying the dharma, likely intending to show that to be an impossibility. The old woman offered to serve Te-shan some mou mou, but only if he could convincingly answer her question. Before asking her question, she let him know that she was familiar with the Diamond Sutra—an important Mahayana sutra that Te-shan had no doubt studied and commented upon. She mentioned a part of the sutra that says the mind of the future cannot be grasped, the mind of the past cannot be grasped, and the mind of the present cannot be grasped. Te-shan affirmed this point, and he must have been stunned just by the fact that this tea-shop-owning old woman knew something he didn't think people like her knew. (Do you see the similarity between Yeshua and the Canaanite woman and Te-shan and the old tea shop woman?) Having thus teed up the unsuspecting scholar, the old lady asked him, "With the mou mou you are ordering, what mind are you seeking to refresh?" Te-shan was completely stumped, and it is said that after hearing her question, he asked for directions to the nearest Zen temple. It was as if Te-shan listened to folk and jazz singer Joni Mitchell's "Both Sides Now"—he realized he really didn't know life at all. The old woman's question was a koan, a relational turning point in not knowing life at all that redirected Te-shan away from his competitive, divisive intention and toward transformative practice.

Yeshua, not considered by most to be a Zen student in the conventional sense, was nevertheless exposed to koanic discourse and became a master in koanic exchange and prophecy. I consider the Sermon on the Mount, the Beatitudes, to be a cyclical-form koan. For example, the first seemingly nonsensical, mind-stopping statement Yeshua makes in that sermon is: "Blessed are the poor in spirit, for theirs is the kingdom of heaven." Then, another seemingly nonsensical, mind-stopping statement: "Blessed are those who mourn, for they will be comforted." We'll examine the Sermon on the Mount in more detail later in this chapter.

Good koans make one stop. When Yeshua and his disciples encountered the Canaanite woman, they did not expect persistence, devotion, and wisdom from a lowly, polytheistic Canaanite woman worthy only of being obliterated. In her determination to recognize Yeshua as spiritual kin, she broke down his psychological barriers, his narcissistic defenses, and his identity-clinging. When that happened, he expressed great generosity toward her child and her, offering her whatever she wanted. Although she thus got what she sought, she simultaneously freed him from prejudice, stinginess, and the delusion of separation. The story of the Caananite woman offers many lessons, including how to recognize both the vulnerability and the strength of people downtrodden by religious and ethnic hatred. This is the power of skillful koanic relationality—with that kind of thinking and being, we can disrupt conventional, dualistic consciousness.

Although koans in their traditional form are unique to the Chinese Chán tradition and its related schools (Japanese, Zen; Vietnamese, *Thiền*; Korean, *Seon* or *Sŏn*), many traditions possess such stories about surprising, even paradoxical exchanges that lead to recognition of our mutuality and vulnerability. These traditions have their main characters—those we've been asked to adore, bow to, pray to, learn from, and worship. These traditions also have stories about those who were deemed unworthy of our relationality—how they were labeled, vilified, unrecognized, and considered suspect. Such "othering" can be for many reasons: they committed heinous crimes, belonged to an "inferior" ethnic group, were old, were women, were polytheistic, had no pastoral authority, and so on. The list can be as long as the delusions we allow our minds to proliferate. I believe the best of these stories illustrate how delusions are created as well as how to develop underutilized human capacities such as altruism, care, compassion, empathy, love, and service. Koanic storytelling has the capacity to help us stop and reorient ourselves toward nurturing the whole, of which we and every tradition are a part. What stories do we tell for the purposes of building our capacities for wholeworking? What stories do we listen to for fulfilling our aspirations to be skilled wholeworkers?

————

One of the most powerful stories coming out of the Christian faith is the Parable of the Good Samaritan—another case of koanic storytelling. One day, a lawyer decided to test Jesus on his knowledge of what the Jewish law has to say in relation to eternalism, so the lawyer asked Jesus how one can have everlasting life. Before moving on to Jesus's answer, let's reflect on this question. The lawyer is asking a question that comes out of humanity's universal existential angst— we want to live forever because we love being alive because we fear not being alive, yet we know we will die one day. Or perhaps our angst comes from the fear that we will live forever, but our eternal life may be one of misery. Jesus, just as many religious leaders today, was posed with an existential question about something he had never experienced—eternal life. He could have attempted an answer, perhaps telling a story that would have allowed the lawyer to imagine himself in it, but Jesus did not. Instead, he decided to answer with a story about a man who had been attacked and left for dead on the road, in public view.

Let's pause to reflect again here because I want to make sure we understand that the Parable of the Good Samaritan pertains to us today. In the summer of 2014, Michael Brown, an unarmed black man-child, was shot by police and left dead on the street in Ferguson, Missouri, for four hours. The body of an eighteen-year-old was on the street for four hours! Oh my God! Before then and since, we have seen many such horrific atrocities that disregard human life and dignity.

Since 2020, there has been a significant uptick in violence against "Chinese-looking" people in the United States, ostensibly because the coronavirus was first located in China; police arrests and killings of unarmed black people; initial governmental neglect of black and brown bodies during the earlier days of the COVID-19 crisis; a white man-child taking a machine gun to a civil rights march in a town he didn't live in and killing two people and seriously injuring another (with the shooter eventually being found not guilty on self-defense grounds); Asian women shot and killed while working in their salons in Atlanta—these and many other stories illustrate our present-day willingness to cause harm and leave people in the streets in their vulnerability.

In the story that Jesus told the lawyer, the victim was lying injured on the street, in plain view for all to see. Two people—a priest and a Levite—saw the vulnerable man. The expectation was that a priest, trained in the rituals that mark rites of passage for others, would stop to assist the man. He did not. Likewise, the expectation was that the Levite, having lived by religious laws, would have grown enough in empathy and sense of duty to stop. Yet he too did not. The Good Samaritan (who I will call Sam), like the priest and the Levite, saw the suffering man (who I will call Jo), went to his aid, and bandaged him. We can imagine that Sam, who was not a medical doctor, made an assessment about Jo's physical wounds and sought to cinch the wounds to ebb the flow of blood. Sam then took the man to an inn for him to have a shelter in which to recover. Sam gave the innkeeper money to care for Jo and promised to visit Jo on his return.

Remember that the lawyer's question to Jesus was, "How can one have everlasting life?" Jesus told the lawyer that the way of relating to one another demonstrated in the Parable of the Good Samaritan is our path to salvation. Compassionate risk-taking relationality is salvation, but we need not be religious leaders to do the work. The work usually comes from the most ordinary, even the most marginalized, people in our society. Mutuality means casting Indra's Net, even and especially when social conventions tell us not to.

How do we embody the spirit of Sam, someone who belonged to a religiously and racially marginalized group? We can embody that spirit by knowing the taste of human dignity and the wholesome desire for wellness and freedom. When anchored deeply in our experience and our bodies, these qualities cannot be manipulated by society's expectations based on our ethnicity, religion, or any categorization. How do dignity, wellness, and freedom transcend societal expectations? Through the wisdom of knowing that these categories possess the quality of emptiness, or no solid mass of unchangeable matter. Jesus's answer to the lawyer, in short, is that creating heaven on earth is our most realistic way to experience the quality of everlasting life. By "quality" I mean living the kind of life that inspires hope in and appreciation for all of humanity. This radical acceptance can be difficult to embrace, and indeed, the lawyer had another question for Jesus: "Who is deserving of this kind of care?" Jesus responded that our neighbor is the one in need. Being a neighbor is not defined by the proximity to which we live near others but by the undeniable fact of our vulnerability. Since we are all vulnerable, and at varying degrees, we are all neighbors, I say spiritual kinfolk, all the time. How radical and intimidating!

As in the Parable of the Good Samaritan, noticing how people are attacked, killed, or left for dead in public view is a litmus test for how we are evolving. On the one hand, we have examples such as that of Michael Brown and of the Asian-descended people who have been attacked in broad daylight, as if the violent perpetrator believed no one would come to their aid. On the other hand, in 2021, a condominium complex in Florida collapsed and there was an immediate rescue effort. We still have the innate capacity to care for those in need, but too often, we choose brutality.

No matter how much people have received spiritual training to attend to others or to live by religious laws, like the priest or the Levite, everyone can make the choice not to live by what they know and to discriminate against others or ignore their plight. We should not be fooled into thinking that our training will protect us from being vulnerable. It is a delusion to believe that anything we've learned will protect us from being attacked, killed, or left for dead. Our mentalities, values, and commitments are labile and subject to exploitation. Herein lies the weakness in the network of mutuality. Perhaps, in such moments of intensity, we are convinced that our own safety is made more secure by ignoring those who are suffering. If people do not learn, through our example, how to attend to vulnerable people, they are likely to be passersby, and perhaps we will be the next ones to experience neglect during a time of extreme vulnerability.

Thankfully, we do have contemporary examples of people acting as Good Samaritans. Recall the several witnesses to the police torture and killing of George Floyd, witnesses who pled with police countless times to release him from the knee-on-the-neck choke. They chose not to be passersby, but active witnesses. They did not abandon Floyd, even as police officers tried to obscure what was happening to him. The witnesses recorded the torture and murder with their cameras and testified in court against the officer. These are modern-day Good Samaritans. If you need encouragement to be a good Sam, read the Good Samaritan law in your state. When doing so, it is likely you will see that your state's law protects its citizens who try to do good by others in their desperation.

The Buddha's Would-Be Murderer:
A Story of Karma and Community

Another parable I draw on for inspiration regarding koanic relationality and spiritual kinship is the Buddhist story of Angulimala. During the Buddha's time, there was a man who had killed many people in his village. He wore a necklace of fingers as proof of his homicidal conquests. Hence his name, Angulimala—which, as noted in the introduction to this book, means "bloody finger garland." He was full of lust for more death, and he wanted to kill the Buddha and add the Buddha's finger to his garland.

One day, Angulimala saw the Buddha walking leisurely in the village, and he began his murderous pursuit. He tried to quickly close in on the Buddha, yet he could not catch him no matter how fast he ran. Angulimala had successfully killed many people, but he could not understand why he could not catch the Buddha, who appeared to be walking slowly and equanimously even though he knew Angulimala was attempting to murder him. Angulimala, in his desperation and failure, called out to the Buddha to stop so he could catch up to him and kill him. The Buddha responded with a koan, saying he had stopped and now Angulimala should stop. Angulimala stopped. He was confused, for he knew neither one of them had stopped moving. What had actually stopped was Angulimala's intent to kill, and this was a liberation.

How did the Buddha not only avoid being murdered but also help to transform his would-be killer's murderousness? Even before Angulimala was freed from his homicidal ways the Buddha did not hate him or reduce him to a person only capable of killing. The Buddha, even as the target of murder, was able to see Angulimala as kin. But being kin doesn't mean we release all of our boundaries with our kinfolk. After Angulimala was released from his murderous intent and repented, the Buddha still made sure to assess whether Angulimala remained a threat to others. Angulimala repented and professed his allegiance to the Buddha and his guidance. What happened in this interpersonal dynamic sparked by koanic relationality? The Buddha mirrored and twinned. The mass murderer had been operating out of a dangerously distorted narcissism. People who have narcissistic personality disorder typically only listen to people they deem superior to themselves. Angulimala bowed down to the Buddha because he perceived the Buddha as superior to himself. This was a skillful means the Buddha used to affect a person who could only be reached through a demonstration of spiritual superiority. Although it's an extreme case, and we don't normally want to risk inflating our own narcissism by trying to demonstrate superiority, we do need to stay on higher moral and ethical ground to bring clarity, purpose, and direction to the transformation of harmful thoughts and behaviors. Not everyone will be in agreement about the transformation project because not everyone will have the same pastoral authority the Buddha had with Angulimala. Likewise, not everyone will have the same understanding of what boundaries are appropriate and when to draw them, as the Buddha did when he said, "I've stopped, now you stop."

When the Buddha respectfully and faithfully told Angulimala to stop trying to enact his wild sense of entitlement to the Buddha's life—something the Buddha had not offered—the Buddha's respect and faith was an act of mirroring, and he also engaged in twinning. The Buddha, in his pastoral authority, told his would-be murderer that he himself had stopped destructiveness. The Buddha admitted he had been destructive! The historical Buddha was named Siddhartha Gautama. He was born into a wealthy warrior caste and thus was taught how to kill. It is possible that the historical Buddha engaged in killing when he was a warrior. He was expected to inherit his father's wealth and caste position. After he left his home to pursue enlightenment, he nearly killed himself by pursuing extreme ascetic practices, including starvation. Siddhartha's destructiveness consisted of the delusion that his wealth made him better than others; the delusion that his wealth and caste protected him from the existential threats we all face; the craving for transcendence from old age, sickness, grief, and death; and the clinging to practices that led him to starvation and near death. When the Buddha said to Angulimala that he had stopped, he had renounced caste status, a legacy of wealth and warriorship, and harmful dualistic thinking. In short, he reduced the craving for and clinging to entitlement. The Buddha's respect for Angulimala was shown in his faith that a murderer could abandon aggression—this amounted to mirroring Angulimala's humanity, which the Buddha was able to sense even underneath Angulimala's rage. We don't have to be pastoral authorities to use mirroring and twinning techniques; however, it is helpful that we transform the destructive parts of ourselves so we can be authoritative when we use mirroring and twinning.

Not everyone would or should do what the Buddha did with Angulimala. I had an experience of doing something similar, but it's not something I recommend to others because it is too risky. When I was in college during my freshmen year, in the winter, I went to a party with my dormitory roommate. I told her not to leave me at the party so I would have someone to walk back home with when I was ready to leave. She agreed. Sometime during the party, she left without telling me, and I had to walk back alone. I remember the coat I wore—an ivory-colored quilted coat with a hood with fake brown and black fur around its edges. Wearing the hood kept my head warm but blocked my peripheral vision. About three hundred feet from the dorm entrance, I could hear someone approaching me from behind. I sped up. About seventy feet from the entrance, the person put their arm around my neck and whispered into my ear that if I didn't go with them, they would cut me. The hood still blocked my vision, but based on the person's deep voice, I understood it was a man who likely wanted to rape me. We live in a rape culture. I froze. In retrospect, I don't believe a whole minute passed. Within that time, I recall noticing that I was in front of the dorm building where I could see many windows. I could scream and maybe someone would hear me. Perhaps I could fight him off. I knew I didn't want to go with him, and in my young racing mind I recall saying to myself, "I don't want to be raped." Actually, I feared living with the aftermath of being raped. I whispered to the assailant, "You'll have to cut me because I'm not going with you." In retrospect, I liken this fear and choice to the fear and choice faced by the fictional character Sethe in Toni Morrison's book *Beloved*. In that book, Sethe kills her own child rather than subjecting her to the violent white rage and mobbery Sethe had endured. I didn't know if the little girl in me could live with the rage of rape. After I told him he'd have to cut me, he released me and ran in the opposite direction. I watched him run and I tried to get a description, but was not able to.

Telling a violence-threatening criminal to go ahead and commit the crime was a spontaneous koanic response. Although this response wouldn't be appropriate for everyone in that situation, I use my story to illustrate the real-life possibility that through koanic attitude, we may be able to help others reduce the extreme dualistic consciousness that can produce violent tendencies, but I reiterate that this experience is not to be taken as advice.

Another aspect of Angulimala's story that I find important is the way in which he was integrated into the Buddha's community. After Angulimala pledged his allegiance to the Buddha, the Buddha, without asking permission from the monks, brought Angulimala to live in their community. This caused a disturbance because Angulimala's reputation preceded him and because he had killed people the monks knew. The monks accosted him and Angulimala suffered physical and psychic harm. Somehow, he thought the monks would treat him with the grace the Buddha had treated him with. The Buddha advised Angulimala to stay in the community for his transformation. That transformation from mass murderer to spiritual adept would include receiving the karma, the cause and effect, of his past violent acts. In short, Angulimala had to take responsibility for the harm he'd committed and receive the karmic consequences.

Despite the monks' violent and retributive behavior, the Buddha helped restore Angulimala back into the community as a shining jewel in Indra's Net. Although it doesn't always get attention, this communal aspect is also present in the other stories we've looked at in this chapter. The Canaanite woman insisted that she be a part of Yeshua's community, and in turn, she affirmed his place in a global and cosmic community by turning his prejudice into generosity. The Samaritan took the injured man to an inn for care and the innkeeper cared for him, restoring him back into a community. That is what radical self-compassion can look and feel like—being the past perpetrator while on the present road to redemption, even through the difficulty of accepting what's coming to you due to the karma of your actions. This path entails being a witness to it all while also protecting others and yourself from future harm. Maybe coming face-to-face with one's karmic consequences reduces narcissistic tendencies. We never really escape the conditions we create because the Network is inescapable. Thus, we can, in mutuality, face the conditions we've created and transform them for the good of the whole. Or we can live our lives on the run, in delusion, until we get caught in the Net.

These stories have resonance with concepts from the contemporary restorative justice movement, which facilitates safe dialogue between victims and offenders and attempts to reach mutual understanding and meaningful resolution. The United States uses its largely unforgiving (ironic in a country that identifies with Christianity), profit-motivated, massive prison industrial complex as a way of discouraging future crimes, but in doing so, it also perpetuates the dehumanization of people who have committed crimes or were successfully prosecuted (guilty or not) for committing crimes. For those who believe in this kind of punishment, the anticipated impact on long-term prisoners is not the restoration of their humanity (as occurred through Malcolm X's relationship with the Nation of Islam founder Elijah Muhammad) but their near-to-eternal or eternal incarcerated damnation (and there is embedded Christian theology to support this).

Long-term prisoners caught in this system are forced to work for a degrading pittance. Some critics of the system, like writer and civil rights activist Michelle Alexander in her book *The New Jim Crow* (2010), call it another form of legalized segregation. The journalist Douglas A. Blackmon has referred to it as "slavery by another name"—the title of his 2008 book on the topic. Whatever the prison industrial complex is compared to, it is in need of restorative justice reforms because many of those currently caught in its grip if given the right conditions and supported by nurturing and skilled people, could be restored. Ironically and unfortunately, the way we punish people in the United States today often makes them more like Angulimala on his rampage. What would it look like for us as a society to learn how to act with the Buddha's composure and equanimity toward those who have committed crimes? "I have stopped, and now you should stop."

The Sermon on the Mount and
the Ethic of Universal Kinship

I see parallels between the stories of the Good Samaritan, the Canaanite woman, and Angulimala as they relate to koans, kinship, and compassion. Koanic relating is relational risk-taking congruent with the Noble Eightfold Path's teachings on Right Intention and Right Action, all informed by compassion at the core. Compassion is the feeling that reminds of us our mutuality. Regional, religious, gender, and moral differences need not prevent the feeling of compassion and thus kinship. It is possible to recognize that it is the vulnerable, our neighbor, who in the expression of the power they still possess reminds us of our impulses to separate ourselves from them and others because of what they represent (the terror of everyone's vulnerability and fragility). Through this recognition, we can grow in our capacity to see them as kin and act as kin toward them.

We adopt each other again and again. All adoptions need not be long-term. Even brief relief like that offered by the Samaritan, Yeshua, and the Buddha may be enough for that particular moment, but such experiences of relief also offer the possibility of ripple effects throughout Indra's Net. For example, the lawyer posed a question to Jesus and Jesus replied that the lawyer should do what the Samaritan did—serve others. The Canaanite woman asked for healing for her child and ultimately received it—and the disciples watched and took the scene as a religious model. The Buddha not only helped Angulimala cease his murderous rage but also brought him into the monastic community to live with others. Thus, each of these stories, though focused in one sense on the interpersonal interactions of the main characters, has a lesson about communal impact. We can think interpersonally, but our civilizing task is to allow ourselves to be informed and transformed from the interpersonal to the communal, from the delusion that family is only defined by genetic markers to the experience of all our neighbors as kin.

Another way of putting it is that we need to work on transcending the individual self-template—which we can do, in part, by living by the Platinum Rule. One of my major sources of inspiration for this view of transcendence is Jesus's Sermon on the Mount—a collection of koanic sayings and teachings made by Jesus in the New Testament. There is much more in the sermon than I can discuss here, so for our purposes, I will mostly focus on Jesus's "kingdom on earth" teachings.

Jesus had returned from a long period of fasting and contemplation in the Judaean Desert and crowds of people had begun to follow him as he traveled and preached around Galilee. The group then gathered on a mountain. On the top of the hill, Jesus said to the crowd something that should make many of us, Christian or not, deeply ponder. He cautioned against oaths—the taking of oaths, the defending of oaths, the imposition of oaths, and not holding people accountable for these behaviors. What did Jesus mean by "oaths"? He meant making a promise *in the name of God* for something that is only in God's realm—having the arrogance, that is, to think one knows and can enforce God's will on Earth. Since mobbery in the United States is sometimes enacted by religious zealots under the auspices of their oaths, we need to think about our attraction to charismatic oath-oriented leaders. They cannot keep their promises because they cannot bind God to those promises. Please ponder this very deeply. Differentiation and individuation allow us to see the hubris in this phenomenon and back away. It will be difficult or impossible to treat others as kin if we feel ourselves oath-bound to views or actions with which others disagree.

Jesus, on the hill, wanted the people to know the end of suffering through the end of craving, or lust, as well as the end of defensiveness. He told them not to be defensive, even in the face of evil, violence, theft, coercion, or need. The opposite of defensiveness is non-aggression and generosity. This is not a doormat posture but a posture of healthy boundaries, for to be a person of non-aggression means no aggression against yourself!

Jesus spoke on the hill to just one group of people, but he reminded them that they belong to a network. This connection can be one of mutuality or of brutality, and I believe Jesus trusted in the bedrock reality of the Network when he said that enemies should be loved and persecutors should be cared for. His message was that we all share in the experience of the nature that nourishes and sustains us and, importantly, if we discriminate against those we don't deem as our blood relatives or see as family, then we are imperfect in our love and should strive for a more perfect, non-discriminating love. Doing so is what makes us, like Jesus, children of God. And it is non-discriminating love, rather than the taking, asserting, defending, and enforcing of oaths, that will produce not a "kingdom" but a "kin-dom" of peace on earth.

Jesus also adjured his listeners to not be anxious about obtaining their basic needs because anxiety does not produce anything. He pointed to the many creatures in nature that have what they need—birds, flowers, grasses. Those who seek God first, he said, will have what they need and they will know to be mindful of the present day, not the future, because the future will bring another set of things to be anxious about. I don't believe calming oneself and putting God first leads to everyone having their basic needs met instantaneously, as populations of religiously devoted people are literally starving to death. But calming oneself can lead to creativity and faith in one's ability to connect with others to have those basic needs sought after and potentially met. If resources are available and accessible, and if we see each other as the Samaritan saw Jo, as the Buddha saw Angulimala, as the Canaanite woman saw Yeshua, and as Yeshua saw humanity's existential suffering, then the equitable distribution of resources may flow more naturally.

Keeping the network of mutuality dynamic and fluid involves recognizing that the basic needs we have are the basic needs of others. Suffering tends to cease when we move from craving to giving—bloody fingers to fragrant flowers. You can pause to feel the energy of craving, the repetitive if not compulsive fixation on getting, and then the release from that energy when you bring to your imagination the act of giving the very thing you've been craving. Please take a moment to feel the sensations. How do you feel as you imagine the joy in giving and the other person receiving?

The network of our mutuality is strengthened by the recognition of the fact of our shared global, universal, and cosmic realities. This recognition can go a long way toward the resolution of opposite positions we hold in our minds and in our lived experiences. For example, for now and the foreseeable future, we are all going to live on the same planet, in the same solar system. The earth will rotate based not on our will but on the cosmic power of how things are. With this acceptance, can we let go of the delusion that we can control everything? If you believe so, contemplate Jesus's teaching on the reasons why we privilege material wealth. He told the crowd to examine their hearts, locate what they really treasure, see the connection between their heart's desire and what they adore, then see if they have placed material wealth (idolizing) over God's love and creation. He reminded them that one cannot serve both. That is not to be taken to mean that

God-serving people cannot have wealth but to mean, at the end of the day, we must choose to be devoted to love and creation over wealth accumulation—to create heaven on earth. The shortest path to heaven is through serving others. Paradoxically, when we serve specific others, we serve the whole community. When we serve the whole community, we serve the cosmos. When we serve the cosmos, we serve creation and creative impulses. For some, when we serve others, we serve God.

AFFIRMATION
We and I belong

There is no "I" without "we" and no "we" without "I." Feel into that reality. Over time we develop a necessary I-sense as part of the normal human developmental process of becoming aware of our discrete bodies and brains. This awareness supports normal differentiation. Being "we" supports the I-sense, and the I-sense, when properly deployed, reminds us of the we-sense. An overactive I-sense promotes delusions of separateness and illusions of total specialness. An overactive we-sense undermines freedom and agency. You can balance both senses to remember that we and I, you and me, belong. We and I belong.

5

The Book of Job

Self-actualization through Community

In Louisville, at the corner of Fourth and Walnut, in the center of the shopping district, I was suddenly overwhelmed with the re- alization that I loved all these people, that they were mine and I theirs, that we could not be alien to one another even though we were total strangers.

—Thomas Merton

I was once asked to speak at a church, one of whose congregants was named Tonel (not their real name, and I will not reveal their gender). Tonel had attempted suicide several times because they were challenged by a condition called borderline personality disorder (BPD). BPD is marked by many symptoms, including emotional dysregulation challenges that can become so intense that the person with BPD engages in a variety of self-harm activities to relieve themselves of mental pain. Tonel's religious community knew that Tonel had suffered intensely and was receiving mental health care treatment, but they did not believe Tonel would be healed through anything other than prayer. For this reason, they regularly laid hands on Tonel, hoping Tonel would heal, but also sent Tonel the message that psychiatry, psychotherapy, and pastoral counseling were futile. Tonel, downtrodden, repeatedly and unsuccessfully told them that prayer alone was futile. As a response to Tonel's desperate plea to their minister, Tonel and the minister asked me to speak at their church about mental illness, BPD, and how it can be treated, in part, through mindfulness. I accepted the invitation out of compassion for Tonel, but I was nervous about how I and my presentation would be received.

I decided to teach, not preach, from the Book of Job, which is in the Ketuvim ("Writings") section of the Hebrew Bible and in the Old Testament of the Christian Bible. The Book of Job is my favorite Bible story about suffering and healing. I know that many people are familiar with the story, but even most of those who are familiar with it have not read it or have not read it carefully and critically from beginning to end. So was the case with Tonel's religious community. Like many others, folks in this community read the beginning of the story where Job is deprived of all that is precious to him, then they skipped to the end where God restores Job twofold. They understood the story to mean, "If you believe in God's goodness, and you're patient, God will give you whatever you've lost and more."

This reading of the Book of Job is the predominant one in popular Christian culture, but I think it reduces this rich parable to one tragic cliché: remain faithful to God, even in tragedy, and God will restore you twofold. When I read the Book of Job, I see much more. I see a story in which relationships need to be restructured through humility and forgiveness, and I think we get the bottom line all wrong—the blessing is not the restoration of things but the restoration of community that was really always there. This is why the Book of Job is one of my greatest inspirations for how we can unlearn and relearn how to be in community.

Job was a pillar of his community and an exemplar of the good life. He was devoted to God, his wife, and his children, and he was wealthy and generous within his community. God, having been told by Satan that Job was only devoted because God had given him a family and wealth, tested Job by letting Satan inflict as much suffering as he could without killing him, foremost by killing his children. Having failed to turn Job against God, Satan cursed Job with boils, and then Job's wife tried to drive a wedge between him and God. Job, even in his pain, suffering, grief, and illness, continued to praise God.

When Job's children were killed and his wealth was destroyed, his friends felt they knew what to do—they would sit with him for seven days and seven nights in silence. This is the Jewish custom called shiva. Our communities have customs for how to attend to another in pain. Bring your custom with you. If you don't know the custom, go anyway, make yourself available, and ask what is needed. There may be no answer. Keeping watch, being in vigil, or being a witness is sometimes the only thing to do. Job's friends initially acted in mutuality, and we can too.

Job sat in silence for the customary amount of time, but when time was up, he proclaimed he wished he had never been born. The suffering Job faced would be enough to make nearly anyone not want to live, and when that desire for non-existence is combined with isolation, alienation is soon to follow. Upon seeing him in his trauma and hearing that sitting shiva had not cured him of it, Job's friends felt alienated from him and began to question and oppose him.

Clearly, Job did not meet his friends' expectations. What did they expect? That Job would be well after seven days and nights of silence in their presence? Why did they expect that? Perhaps because others had been able to grieve enough in that time to move forward in their lives. Maybe because we believe in the rules given to us by religious authorities. In any case, what other people experience and whatever rules are promulgated, no one has the magical foresight to anticipate how another human being will respond to even a single tragedy, much less multiple traumatic tragedies in quick succession.

Job's friends turned on him because they had a different cosmology than Job (we'll return to the subject of cosmologies in chapter 7). They believed God killed Job's children, robbed him of his wealth, and sickened him all because God was displeased with Job. They could not fathom any other reason why God would let these tragedies occur. Job assured them that he was right with God, and he persisted in voicing this belief. Their cosmologies collided to such a degree that his formerly compassionate friends began to see Job, once the most pious person they knew, as blasphemous. They believed that Job couldn't know the mind of God well enough to know that God would not do this to him. So, they argued back and forth, and as they did so, Job became sicker and sicker with what we know today as complicated grief, depression, anxiety, paranoia, obsessiveness, compulsion, and suicidal ideation. In all, Job had a religious and existential problem.

Before he was afflicted, Job was humble in his righteousness. But after he was repeatedly accused of not being righteous, he became defensive, repeatedly asserting to his friends that his relationship with God was solid. Job's friends interpreted his defensiveness as religious arrogance. Even God saw that Job had crossed the line, so God gave Job a good dose of humility by asking him to contemplate whether he'd been with God since the beginning of time and creation.

Of course, Job had not been, and he used his contemplative capacity to hear the question, ponder it, and readjust. Job emerged from his defensiveness to admit that he didn't really know what he was talking about when he spoke so confidently about the nature and will of God. We should take heed. Quieting himself not only helped Job drop his defensiveness but also apparently had a soothing impact on the community such that the unnecessary and unproductive arguing ceased. Contemplation supports community building and maintenance because it helps us keep our egos in check. Through contemplation, Job was able to release his obsessiveness and compulsiveness and receive God's instructions to forgive his friends who had lambasted him.

Reading the Book of Job, I take the lesson that Job's healing came through a kind of surrender. In addition to contemplating God's question, Job heard from a young witness named Elihu, who asserted to Job that stillness must come first. Job took heed, entered stillness, and allowed himself to be changed by stillness. When he did so, it not only helped him but also helped reverse the strain that had come upon his relationships and opened the door to a restructuring of the community through community commitment, effort, and forgiveness. Job, a pillar of the community, had been reduced to a downtrodden victim, and the structure of the community became distorted. God demanded that the community restore Job, because of his righteousness, to his proper place—but that was only able to happen through the restoration of mutuality between Job and his community.

Seeing Tonel's Essence

Sitting shiva did not cure Job. The lesson here is that we cannot expect any of our religious customs, rituals, beliefs, or even the presence of our spiritual kin, to cure traumatic events. Even if we believe in miracles, we do not possess the omniscience to know if and when those miracles will happen—or how. Truly being in mutuality entails knowing we have no control over outcomes, and thus we endeavor to adopt an attitude of acceptance of what is, along with the ethic of refraining from imposing a particular outcome or timetable on others. This posture is a way of understanding grace. To extend the posture or attitude of grace means we release our expectations and refrain from imposing our demands. Extending such grace, I believe, is what we need to contribute to a community that leans toward mutuality rather than brutality.

This interpretation of Job's story is what I talked about in Tonel's church on the day of my visit. I shared my view that the Book of Job is not about one man but about humanity itself; that grief and trauma are not the same thing; and that Job, representing humanity, suffers from depression, anxiety, obsession, compulsion, religious problems, existential crises, and suicidality—even though God loved him and he loved God. And I said that Tonel, in their suicidality, was no different from Job or the rest of humanity.

As I worked my way through the story, I pointed out that laying on of hands—one of the main ways the church community was trying to support Tonel—was a ritualized practice in being good spiritual kin. It was akin to how Job's friends earnestly sat shiva with him when they sat with him in silence for seven days and seven nights after his children were killed. In saying this, I was trying to communicate to Tonel's fellow church members that it was good for them to offer this kind of support, but I was also opening the door to the idea that it would not have the desired outcome of curing Tonel's BPD and suicidality. In this community, I was treading, perhaps stomping, onto dangerous theological ground when I said that Job's friends didn't save him from suicidality and that laying on of hands would not cure Tonel. I could see people's eyes bore into me, their facial muscles tensing. The tone and pace of our dialogue changed from engaged to tepid to frustrated, but out of compassion for Tonel, I continued.

When Job's friends turned on him, accusing him and his children of being disobedient, Job repeatedly protested that he and God were one. Human oneness with divinity is a common theme and aspiration in many religious and spiritual traditions. It is as if recognizing one's truest, purest essence is vital to staying connected and ethical. I wanted Tonel's essence to be revealed as whole and good in the midst of their profound struggle for mental health, not in spite of it.

As we made our way to the end of Job's story, I said that, though God, in the end, grants Job a new family and wealth, the Bible is silent on whether Job was healed of suicidality. Translating this uncertainty to Tonel's situation, I suggested the community should give medical, psychotherapeutic, and spiritual counselors a chance to help Tonel heal. The folks did not jump up exclaiming, "Halleluiah!" and I did not expect them to. They were polite as I brought my presentation and plea to a close. The next day, the pastor called me to say that he supported everything I said and told the congregation so, but I would not be invited back to the church for a part two. I understood. On behalf of Tonel and hopefully others in the congregation who were suffering, I did my job—out of compassion. My hope is that the congregation began to see Tonel differently, not as just a downtrodden person with no knowledge and wisdom of their own, but as a person in need of a different kind of spiritual kinship, one that would not interfere with strategies that have been proven to be helpful. Like the Canaanite woman and her child, Tonel had been stigmatized, their full humanity rejected. The power of stigma is that it tarnishes our perceptions. Tonel had been asking their religious community to understand what they were going through and not get in the way of healing, but they could not hear Tonel without a pastoral counseling intervention (backed up by their pastor) that was disruptive of their normal ways of perception and spiritual practice.

CONTEMPLATION
Elihu's Stillness

As noted above, in Job's story a critical turning point happens when Elihu insists that stillness comes first. It is with this intervention that Elihu begins the process of casting Indra's Net toward Job, inviting his awareness that he remains in the realm of abundance. Let's pause for a moment from the cognitive experience of reading, understanding, interpreting, meaning-making, reflecting, and trying to remember what you just read. Let go of the impulse to agree or disagree with what you just read. Please take a few deep breaths. Rest as your body settles into stillness.

Now, recall a memory of someone who suffered terribly and asked for your help, but you resisted. Inhale and exhale. Pause. Hold the memory. Any judgment, confusion, self-righteousness, or feeling of being under-resourced?

Check the sensations in your body. Inhale and exhale. Did they withdraw their request after you resisted? Inhale, exhale, pause, and check sensations. Any wonderment, relief, shame, guilt, or lament? Did they persist? Pause. If they persisted, how did you feel? Inhale, exhale, check sensations. Was there any annoyance? Do you remember if and when your resistance broke? Inhale, exhale, check sensations. Pause.

What was the final straw that broke your camel-back defense? Do you remember how that felt? How does it feel now as you recall the moment? Inhale, exhale, check sensations. Pause.

What can be learned from inhaling, exhaling, pausing, and checking sensations? Those seemingly brief temporal moments are pregnant with cosmic possibilities because they can release us from habituated personality patterns infused with tension, resistance, defenses, hatred, narcissism, group over-identification, stigmas, and totalizing, and open us to the world of relationships and resources.

Communitas: Applying the Lessons of Job to Our Collective Situation

I would like to introduce the term *communitas*, which is a Latin word used in Catholicism. I understand it to mean "community" but also something more—a community of healing. *Communitas* means "being-with-unity." It is a state of being together with others, with an inclination toward connecting and an agreeableness around coexisting, which involves developing our understanding of what it takes to coexist. It is a proclivity toward harmony and compromise, thinking about the well-being of the self in tandem with the well-being of the whole. People in the mind state of communitas prefer wholeworking to networking, sensing that they will receive plenty of benefit from this communal mutuality even though certain occasions will entail the discomforts of refraining from egotism. One could argue that a healthy community requires a level of selflessness from its members because attending to others, especially those in need, is a crucial ingredient of community life.

Let's continue looking at the Book of Job as a way of examining what communitas could mean in the conditions we are living in now. As I consider how Job's friends initially became alienated from him,

I think that, as we attempt to be good spiritual kin—embodying the loving Jesus, for those of us who identify as Christians—we should also examine within ourselves how much of the judgmental and wrathful God we carry within our psyches and worldviews. Our sense of the teeter-totter of God's essential nature as punisher or as nurturer impacts how we are with people in religious and spiritual distress. Job, his suffering, and his understanding of suffering represent this heart-wrenching tension. Phrased as a question, it would be: "If God is loving, why is this happening to me?"

Job is a representative of humanity and his story reflects the fact that we all experience the harshness of life differently. We often do not appreciate the ways people express their pain, but in community, we learn to be nonjudgmental so that people can authentically express pain and relief, joy and sorrow, disappointment and surprise. There is no emotion that exists outside community and no healing that takes place outside community. Community is where both violence and peace occur.

Job, as humanity, always had religious and existential problems. Our communities always have religious and existential problems— this is part of the human condition, and turning on each other because of the human condition is foolish. Turning on each other does not eliminate the pains of our religious and existential situation—it exacerbates them! By not extending Job a posture of grace, his friends increased his suffering. They got locked in theological posturing about the extent of Job's knowledge of God. I have written about Job as representing humanity, but his friends also represent humanity, and all together they represent a community divided by religious differences. Captured by their ideas about how Job was supposed to be, they got so involved with arguing about religious differences that they lost sight of opportunities for healing, until the young witness Elihu intervened.

We need to look very closely at how our disappointments in others get projected onto others, as if it is their responsibility to meet our expectations in addition to contending with the pain and suffering they are already experiencing. Compassion means not heaping the fulfillment of our expectations onto the sufferer. We need to take responsibility for healing our own disappointments. Instead of offering those who are suffering our expectation that they stop suffering, we can offer them our presence as compassionate witnesses to their suffering.

In communitas, we desperately need witnesses. Not everyone starts with the same capacity to witness. As noted earlier in this book, I was for many years unable to witness death, and I needed time, spiritual kin, and training to develop that capacity. Not all people have worked on transforming the personality issues that prevent them from witnessing others, which includes working toward a nondiscriminatory view of humanity. For example, it is said that Siddhartha Gautama nearly killed himself while engaging in spiritual practices that he thought would save him from the vicissitudes of life. Consequently, he learned that all people, no matter their religious practices, would experience aging, illness, separation, and death.

Let's look more closely at Elihu's role in Job's story. Elihu observed what happened between Job and his friends. He watched, listened, and assessed that Job would not heal until he could find quietude. Job became a contemplative, at least briefly, when Elihu told him that he would not get the peace, joy, and contentment he desired if he kept engaging in the argument he was having with his friends. Job, once a pillar in the community, got to a place where he was no longer a contributing member, not because of his losses and illnesses, but because he and his friends were distracted from what was important. Elihu played a crucial role in helping Job reconnect to his capacity for contemplation—which, as we have seen, allowed Job to begin the process of surrendering and inviting his community into repair.

Witnesses help us understand the truth of our lives, even if it is hard to bear. Unbiased witnesses help us understand the impact we have on others, and they play a key part in healing wounds, righting wrongs, or meting out justice. Witnesses who have the fortune of being "outside" the circumstance, who are not taking sides and are not particularly invested in the outcome, are well poised for reporting the events untarnished. But I don't want to make it sound like witnessing is always straightforward—it can be hard to know how one's witnessing is affecting a situation, and there can be a tension between being a witness and being a snitch.

I remember being shocked when someone told me that they saw a crime being committed but didn't want to tell the police because they didn't want to be a snitch. They did not want to become an agent of the police force, known by many to be a brutal force. This is an ethical dilemma that is very difficult to resolve for people who are constantly or feel constantly surveilled by police officers. If someone wants to support the well-being of their community and sees crimes being committed, but has good reason to distrust the police, what are they to do? We certainly need to weigh the severity of the crime against what we know to be supportive of a healthy community. For example, do we need more people in prison for drug use offenses? No. Do people who shoot our children dead need to be prevented from killing other children? Absolutely! How do we best do that? I don't know, but hatred can be transformed into the path of love, and among my sources of hope are the prison chaplains doing this work.

When I lived in Oakland, California, in 2007, we organized a public collective mourning event the day before Mother's Day. We called it Mother's Morning-Mourning, and we did it because so many young people had been shot dead. We believed these mothers' grief should be acknowledged, and we believed that their grief and calls for peace could convince some people to refrain from violence against children and inspire young people to renounce violence. Did it work? We worked. We worked to shift the culture, and that is our never-ending work to do. Whatever cultural experiments we engage in, we can become wholesome witnesses by letting our witness be the medicine for another's healing. This is communitas.

Although we can never know for certain in advance that our witnessing will be helpful, I believe a contemplative lifestyle lays the groundwork for improving our intuition in this regard. Having a contemplative practice can remind us of the fact that we are related to one another and that there are gifts we can offer to one another. Contemplation can hone our awareness of when something is off-kilter in our communities, giving us the information we need to take action. Restructuring our communities for the good of the entire community, not just for the restoration of one person, is an act of selflessness. To put the good of the whole before the wants of one individual is wholeworking.

The contemplative lifestyle supports wholeness because it is about wholeness—attuning the mind, body, and heart-mind to cognize beyond individuality without excluding individuality. It is a practice in humility and belonging. A contemplative lifestyle involves simplifying one's life by identifying mental distractions and reformulating our relationship with those distractions. For example, if you find you have recurring thoughts about something or someone you are attracted to, find ways to reduce the occurrence of those thoughts. If you are immersed in many relationships with people who consistently vex you, reduce the number of interactions you have with them. If you are attracted to drama, investigate what attracts you to drama and learn to find drama as a distraction itself. If you find that you spend so much time thinking about yourself that you do not think about the welfare of others, turn your attention away from yourself to devote a little more attention to others. If you spend a lot of time and money shopping for things you don't need, find out what you're avoiding paying attention to by fixating on shopping. There are many ways we consciously and unconsciously choose to do things that don't bring us peace, joy, ease, contentment, or concentration.

It is said in Buddhism that there are four kinds of people:

1. People who have unwholesome wishes but do not understand the true nature of their unwholesomeness
2. People with unwholesomeness who understand the true nature of their unwholesomeness
3. People who do not have unwholesomeness and do not understand the true nature of their not having unwholesomeness
4. People who do not have unwholesomeness and understand the true nature of not having unwholesomeness

As I mentioned previously, unwholesomeness stems from roots of greed, hatred, and delusion, as well as killing, stealing, sexual misconduct, lying, harsh speech, gossip, covetousness, general ill will, wrong view, or ignorance. To live more harmoniously in community, through meditation, contemplation, and practice, we try to go from being people who have unwholesome wishes and operate from that unwholesomeness to people who become aware of our unwholesomeness, understand why unwholesomeness is there, refrain from projecting that unwholesomeness onto others, and commit to renouncing unwholesomeness as a way of life. Becoming a person who prefers wholesomeness supports our ability to be witnesses.

Practicing Transformative Pilgrimage, Whether You Leave Home or Not

I mentioned at the beginning of this book that my parents bought a house in a neighborhood near the end of white flight. That was 1966 in Indianapolis, Indiana. Today, in many urban neighborhoods around the United States, white flight has taken an about-face and is now called gentrification. White flight deprived and deprives neighborhoods of human and monetary assets; gentrification returns human and monetary assets but with economic pressures that make it difficult for those still in the community to stay. My point in mentioning this is that communities, like everything else, are changeable. Can we be changeable with a being-with-unity, communitas mentality so wealthier people don't leave out of fear? And if they return, can they return in a way that will allow those already there to stay if they want to? Of course.

Whenever greed, hatred, and delusion are at the root of how we build community, then no matter whether we stay, leave, or return, we will perpetuate cycles of poverty and extreme wealth inequality that obscure the reality of our shared humanity and pit us against each other in class and caste warfare. How can we move past the delusion that our appearance and our economic situation actually mean we are of different kinds of human species? The pursuit of economic gain at the expense of the well-being of others (unrestrained capitalism) is another form of brutality.

Many of the cultural practices and assumptions that support zero-sum capitalism are so deeply embedded that they will not be easily changed. To move wholesomely from brutality to mutuality may require that many of us experience a pilgrimage of one sort or another—a transpersonal experience that can only be had by dwelling with people unlike ourselves. I am moved by the transformations Gandhi underwent through such experiences, which we'll look at in the next chapter. Likewise by Malcolm X's transformative insight when he was making hajj, or pilgrimage, to Mecca. While there, he had an overwhelming, first-hand transpersonal experience of humanity that ran contrary to the anti-white rhetoric he was taught to believe and had himself professed. He wrote:

> My vocabulary cannot describe the new mosque [in Mecca] that was being built around the Ka'aba, a huge black stone house in the middle of the Grand Mosque. It was being circumambulated by thousands upon thousands of praying pilgrims, both sexes, and every size, shape, color, and race in the world. . . . My feeling here in the House of God was numbness. My *mutawwif* (religious guide) led me in the crowd of praying, chanting pilgrims, moving seven times around the Ka'aba. Some were bent and wizened with age; it was a sight that stamped itself on the brain.[1]

After his pilgrimage, Malcolm X became El-Hajj Malik El-Shabazz, which means, roughly, "the one who made Islamic pilgrimage in Mecca and became a generous, noble royal." Shabazz maintained that racism in the US was evil, but he renounced considering all white people as devils. He proceeded to build additional Muslim movements in the United States.

Of course, mass pilgrimages do not always result in such a positive view of humanity and one's place in it. Many injurious and deadly stampedes have occurred during mass pilgrimages in different religious traditions and different countries, and I see these as examples of mobbery overtaking the crowd. Even if many people in the crowd hold the best of intentions, the vibrational quality of the crowd can turn it into a violent melee. If one is not drawn to be in the midst of such large groups or cannot go on pilgrimage for other reasons such as family responsibilities, lack of paid vacation, lack of resources, or lack of connection to a pilgrimage tradition, I think it is still possible to aspire toward the transformative experience of pilgrimage in one's contemplative life. To me, this means creating a thirst for wisdom with others who also have that aspiration while not actively trying to separate ourselves from the worldly.

There is the concept of a "staycation"—refraining from the routine of a job but not leaving town, enjoying the ordinariness of home life. Can we have a "stay-pilgrimage"? I learned about the Trappist monk and author Thomas Merton when I was a Buddhist graduate student at the Catholic university Holy Names University. Merton, who also wrote about Catholicism and Zen, had a stay-pilgrimage in Louisville, Kentucky, where he lived at Gethsemani Abbey. Merton had an experience similar to that of Malcolm X in Mecca. Merton wrote:

In Louisville, at the corner of Fourth and Walnut, in the center of the shopping district, I was suddenly overwhelmed with the realization that I loved all these people, that they were mine and I theirs, that we could not be alien to one another even though we were total strangers . . .

This sense of liberation from an illusory difference was

such a relief and such a joy to me that I almost laughed out loud... And if only everybody could realize this! But it cannot be explained. There is no way of telling people that they are all walking around shining like the sun... If only we could see each other that way all the time. There would be no more war, no more hatred, no more cruelty, no more greed.... But this cannot be seen, only believed and "understood" by a peculiar gift.[2]

Some people, like El-Hajj Malik El-Shabazz, need to leave their communities to understand that we are all together in this thing called life, but some of us can experience what Thomas Merton experienced right at home, during a stay-pilgrimage. How? Perhaps a reflection on the Platinum Rule might be helpful. Maybe some lovingkindness meditation would be helpful (we'll explore walking lovingkindness meditation in chapter 7). What about a reflection on the Prayer of St. Francis? How about tonglen? How about surrendering the delusion of separateness?

There are many ways to realize and actualize our belonging to one another. The Buddha moved grove to grove with his followers. What if we were more invitational about including people in our journeys toward the wholesome? Isn't every gathering of humans actually a family reunion? The refusal to recognize ourselves as kin takes a lot of energy, so why not be free of that Wrong View and Effort? We belong to one another regardless of our self-absorption. It is psychologically difficult to transform narcissism, but with people who are willing to learn how to mirror and twin, as Heinz Kohut taught, it will be worth the effort because the reward may be the experience of casting Indra's Net and catching ourselves and each other.

AFFIRMATION

I fulfill cosmic integration by becoming an awakening one

You were born into an ignorance some call "aperspectivalness" (being without a perspective). As your brain functions developed to make simple distinctions (good if it meets your needs, bad if it doesn't), hold memories, and make interpretations and meaning, you gained perspectives—but they were still manifestations of ignorance of the whole world of phenomena of causes and conditions. Aperspectivalness is nothing to be ashamed of—we are all limited. The process of awakening means letting go of the clinging to limited perspectives and wrong views, including the view that you are completely separate from everyone else and the view that "worldlings" can be avoided and segregated. Recognizing and accepting your interrelated self in material and nonmaterial realities, you awaken. I fulfill cosmic integration by becoming an awakening one.

6

Action without Attachment

The Bhagavad Gita and the Lessons of Paradox

Mohandas Karamchand Gandhi, also known as Mahatma Gandhi, was born in India to Indian parents in 1869. He was assassinated in 1948. An incredible journey of a life transpired between those dates. As a child, Gandhi was deeply influenced by his mother's devotional Hinduism and by the veneration of truth and love he found in stories from the Indian classics. His father served in the administration of the British Raj, and Gandhi, like many Indians of his time, thought of India as an important and respected part of the empire and of himself as a British subject. In his late teens and early twenties, he studied law in England and while there saw a different side of European colonial thought. After traveling to South Africa, then also a British colony, in 1893 to practice law, he experienced violent racial discrimination and began to question British colonialism more deeply. Remaining in South Africa until 1914, he went through a significant spiritual conversion, left the practice of law, became an activist and theologian, and led successful nonviolent anti-colonialist movements before returning to India to do the same.

I never grow tired of watching the feature film about Gandhi. After I learned about him, I was so thoroughly impressed by his life that I made my young daughter watch that movie with me every year as she was growing up. Why? I wanted her to know that social change for human rights is possible and that she could find a place in a movement at some point in her life when social change and her participation were needed.

When I learned that Gandhi considered the Bhagavad Gita, one of the thousands of holy scriptures of Hinduism, like his eternal mother, I had to read it. Then I had to read it again and again—it took me at least four times before I began to get it because it begins, shockingly, with the god Krishna telling his devotee Arjuna to murder Arjuna's kinfolk! How could Gandhi—a man who sacrificed so much for the well-being of others in two countries, on two continents, and whose example inspired Rev. Dr. Martin Luther King Jr. and the civil rights movement of the 1960s in the United States—embrace a murderous text like this? I had forgotten at the time that I already knew something, through music, about the love of Krishna and his devotees.

In the 1970s, when I was young and of the record-album-buying age, I bought my first two albums at a garage sale. One was by the Russian composer Sergei Rachmaninoff, which I purchased not because I loved classical music but because I thought he had an interesting face. The other was the *Hair* soundtrack, which I bought because I had a big afro, like the afro on the cover. Little did I know the album would influence me to respect and appreciate Krishna worship. Before purchasing these albums, I had been unintentionally and subliminally "indoctrinated" by my aunt into my own eternal mother: Earth, Wind, and Fire (EWF). My aunt, like my mother, was adopted, and she is just five years older than I am. She told me she first encountered EWF when she was sixteen or seventeen, which means that by age eleven or twelve I was absorbing their songs by osmosis and singing them myself not long after. Their 1973 album *Head to the Sky* includes "Keep Your Head to the Sky," their 1974 album *Open Our Eyes* includes "Devotion," their 1975 album *That's the Way of the World* includes the megahits "Shining Star" and "Reasons," and their many albums thereafter provided and still provide the main spiritual soundtrack of my life. Lyrics such as this one—"You're a shining star / No matter who you are"[1]—sank deep into my mind and heart like mantras. Thus, it was EWF that prepared me to absorb the hippy Broadway soundtrack *Hair*, including its song devoted to Krishna.

I played *Hair* on my little portable turntable so many times one would think I'd have worn the vinyl grooves down to the point where no music was left. I played that album with a kind of religious devotion, as if it was my personal anthem and path to salvation, even though I didn't understand everything (if anything really) that soundtrack was about. What I understood, though, was that I loved listening and singing to the song "Be In—Hare Krishna." So, in my youth I sang and chanted as the grooves wore down:

HARE KRISHNA HARE KRISHNA
KRISHNA KRISHNA HARE HARE
HARE RAMA HARE RAMA
RAMA RAMA HARE HARE...

And there was another song in the atmosphere and my consciousness about being devoted to Krishna. I didn't understand it then either. The late former Beatle George Harrison wrote and recorded "My Sweet Lord" in 1970. I don't remember the year or my age when I first heard and sang this song, but the chorus includes Harrison singing to Krishna as his "sweet lord."

What if I had remembered these songs before reading the Gita? If I had remembered, I'm sure my first and subsequent readings would have been less disturbing because I would have remembered my own singing and chanting HARE KRISHNA even as I was being raised in the United Methodist Church. Given the electricity and love I felt in my body as I sang those songs, I could have intimated that there must be a deeper spiritual meaning to the exchange between Krishna and Arjuna. As it was though, I found the story troubling. The dialogue between Krishna and Arjuna takes place in the middle of a battlefield, with an army on each side poised to fight. Stephen Mitchell translates the scene this way:

> Arjuna saw them standing there: fathers, grandfathers, teachers, uncles, brothers, sons, grandsons, fathers-in-law, and friends, kinsmen on both sides, each side arrayed against the other. In despair, overwhelmed with pity, he said: "As I see my own kinsmen, gathered here, eager to fight, my legs weaken, my mouth dries, my body trembles, my hair stands on end, my skin burns, the bow Gandiva drops from my hand. I am beside myself, my mind reels. I see evil omens. Krishna: no good can come from killing my own kinsmen in battle."[2]

Arjuna laments the probability of mass violence toward innocent people and the violence he is being called to commit against his kin. Krishna responds: "Why this timidity, Arjuna, at a time of crisis? It is unworthy of a noble mind: it is shameful and does not lead to heaven. This cowardice is beneath you, Arjuna: do not give in to it. Shake off your weakness. Stand up now like a man."[3]

I was shocked! How could this book be Gandhi's eternal mother? How could a God who, according to Gandhi, inspired decolonizing liberation also be a God of mobbery? Come again?! I recall having a similar response when I decided to read the Bible from cover to cover, book to book. I was exposed to so much violence that I had to put it down. Many commentators have said that the armies and killing in the Gita are used allegorically, and perhaps that is true. But I find it helpful as well to consider Arjuna as an actual person and consider his situation. What I didn't understand, and still seek to understand more deeply, is that Arjuna, the potential mass murderer of his kin, was caught between warring factions, and his morality, devotion, and spiritual life were being put to the test. I think Krishna was testing Arjuna similarly to how God tested Job. These characters are really being tested by the many difficult and often violent challenges in life—challenges we face in real life today as well. Their pursuit of truth and goodness, represented by their desire to be at one with their gods, ultimately leads them out of self-destruction and mobbery.

One of the ways their gods lead them out of destruction is through koans that are initially quite confusing. In this sense, the Gita's teaching is what I call a long-form koan. Rather than a pithy exchange or story, it presents an epic scene in which paradox is employed to teach an already moral person about the nature of God and how to live in divine accord. The Book of Job is also a long-form koan about teaching an already moral and devoted man, Job, about the nature of God, in that case through cruelly and traumatically depriving him of nearly everyone and everything he loved. The Gita's teaching, like the Sermon on the Mount in the Bible, is a dialectic—pitting opposites against one another to arrive at the truth. Typically, it requires patience and curiosity, especially for people conditioned by strict either-or thinking, before becoming more comfortable with the discomfort that tends to arise when deriving meaning from such challenging stories.

The Gita's teaching is ultimately about how to continue on the path of yoga, wisdom, compassion, and Self-actualization (union with divine substance). Arjuna, through his conversations with Krishna, goes from profound sorrow to bliss. His merger with God is the real "war" being "fought." In the end, the conversation about the mass killing of kinfolk disappears. No physical battle takes place in this version of the Gita, and I take this to mean that one cannot simultaneously be about Self-actualization on the one hand and mobbery and mass murder on the other. Krishna says to Arjuna:

> I am imperishable time . . . the courage of all brave men:
> of the Vrishi clan, I am Krishna;
> of Pandavas, I am Arjuna[4]

Krishna thus affirms his oneness with Arjuna. Imagine you are Arjuna, who has had a long conversation with Krishna about why you don't want to kill others, while Krishna repeatedly encourages you to kill. Then you get to a point in the conversation where Krishna reveals himself to be divine and says he is you! With an open heart, devoted to this creative and all-pervading mystery, your sense of self might change radically. True freedom comes from renouncing violence.

When I was a youth in the United Methodist Church, I once asked my pastor, the late Rev. Jerry Hyde, what he wanted me to call him. Did he want me to call him Jerry, as the adults addressed him, or Rev. Hyde, as I was taught to respectfully address adults? He told me Rev. meant "revered" and that God revered all people, so I was as revered by God as he was, therefore I could call him Jerry. I never called him Jerry, but what he said made a deep impression on me. The lesson he imparted to me in my youth was that we were no different in the cosmos, though there were many obvious differences in age, race, sex, gender, experience, roles, and so on. Fortunately, Rev. Hyde used his pastoral authority in a way that radically and immediately altered my sense of self and possibility. What a profound and miraculous gift! I know he didn't realize at the time how enduring his teaching was, but it saved me, ironically, when Rev. Hyde himself tried to intervene in the expression of my sexual orientation.

In 1992, twenty-three years before gay marriage was legal throughout the United States, Rev. Hyde reached out to me to advise me against the "gay lifestyle." I know that he was under religious pressure and had been called by one of my relatives to save me from myself. In short, he tried to keep me in a heteronormative caste system. His weapon was shame. Eventually, as the marriage equality movement took hold, Rev. Hyde reached out to me of his own volition. He told me that he had felt sorry for many years for having attempted to persuade me to be someone I was not. He said he had learned over the years that I was still revered, and he apologized and asked for forgiveness. Of course, I forgave him immediately because despite his intrusion and shaming, for which I was angry in that moment, he had given me the greatest gift decades earlier—he had told me that we are all revered.

For Rev. Hyde to impart to me that I, even as a pre-teen, was revered by God as much as a pastor is like Krishna saying to Arjuna that they are one. Krishna further shares that their interpenetrating being supports the entire cosmos with just one fragment of its Self. Can we support the entire cosmos with one fragment of ourselves? (I return to the notion of knowing our place in the cosmos in chapter 7.)

Acting without Attachment to Outcomes

We have now seen the paradoxical or koanic nature of Arjuna's situation in the Gita. Is he fighting in a real battle, a spiritual battle, both, or neither? Is Krishna external, internal, both, or neither? Yet the text does not simply linger in these mysteries—it engages numerous topics concerning ethics and right action. It is a spiritual text about yoga and wisdom, and like Gandhi, I take it to be fundamentally about nonviolent Self-actualization. How, then, do yoga and wisdom, according to the Gita, support the path from mobbery to nonviolence? In short, this path involves engaging in necessary actions with no attachment to the fruits of action.

Krishna tells Arjuna that, on the path to Self-actualization, the yoga of devotion is to rejoice in the welfare of others, understanding that they also have the capacity for Self-actualization. Contrary to Krishna's exhortation that Arjuna should kill people, Krishna also tells Arjuna to rejoice in others' welfare. This is koanic—it presents Arjuna with a seemingly unresolvable dilemma that he has to live his way into rather than figure out using logic. Knowing that Arjuna, at this point in the conversation, has not experienced Self-actualization, Krishna reminds Arjuna that even in confusion, one can act without attachment. I understand this from the perspective of the Tao Te Ching:

> The ancient Masters said,
> "If you want to be given everything,
> give everything up."[5]

That's also the essence of what the young witness Elihu told Job—that he wouldn't get anything he wanted until he became still and stopped clinging and craving. How koanic. The Tao Te Ching, the Book of Job, and the Gita all seek to show how clinging and craving cause psychological "uniperspectivalness." In other words, when we seek to belong to or have something or someone that is largely harmful to us, our ability to perceive broadly, with the capacity to recognize and embrace additional truths and thereby embody "multiperspectivalness," is severely diminished. Clinging and craving, or unhealthy attachment, hinders our freedom and deludes our minds into thinking we are separate from everything else that is. To be nonattached, broaden our perspective, is to be better able to mirror loss, untarnished, within Indra's Net.

In Hinduism, Krishna is the god of protection and compassion. His role is like that of Jizo (in Sanskrit, Ksitigarbha), the bodhisattva-protector of children in Zen, and like Christopher, the saint-protector in Catholicism. Krishna appears in a more paradoxical manner than Jizo or Christopher though, telling Arjuna that nonviolence and humility are character traits he should cultivate, even while Krishna is serving as Arjuna's charioteer on a battlefield. How confusing and frustrating this must be for Arjuna! Arjuna stops many times to understand Krishna's long-form koanic dialogue. In a parallel to Buddhism's teachings on how to lessen and relinquish one's attachments to one's sense of self, personality, and identity, Krishna tells Arjuna to learn how to be free from the "I-sense." I understand the I-sense to mean the deluded belief that each one of us is a discrete entity unrelated to others and thus not responsible for others' welfare. It is the opposite of Indra's Net. To be free from the I-sense is to be aware, Self-actualized within the network of promoting mutuality, as pristine of a mirror as possible, not tilting toward brutality. And yet, Arjuna is not on a meditation cushion but on a battlefield—his freedom from the I-sense must come in the midst of intensity, unavoidable choices, and action.

Arjuna wants to know Krishna; Krishna claims he is Arjuna. Therefore, Arjuna doesn't know himself. Krishna persistently tests Arjuna until he gets there—through complete devotion. Initially, Arjuna was not ready to know Krishna, and Krishna was not ready to tell Arjuna how to know him, but they get to a place in their dialogue where Krishna says a devotee is one who understands that knowledge and the object of knowledge are inseparable. He puts it like this: this body is the field of existence itself and the observer of all that happens within the field is the Knower. Krishna, therefore, is the Knower that resides in the body-as-existence-itself. Knowledge is paradoxically within and outside what we take to be existence, and when this is understood, a devotee is ready to understand Krishna. The development of our spiritual lives depends, in part, on contemplating the myriad ways we and others come to know what we know. This is critical to understanding how the network of our mutuality has the potential to save us from being brutally destructive—we become able to see the Self in the self and better able to cast Indra's Net.

He who sees that the great Lord
is equally in all beings.
Deathless when every being
Dies—that man sees truly.[6]

We share the same source, same elements. This source and elemental nature exist beyond the death of our bodies, and when we understand this, we can move beyond reflecting each other in the mundane sense of "what I see in the mirror must look like me to reflect back who I am." This type of mundane reflection lacks the depth to respect difference— in its insecurity, it can only tolerate sameness. When we find ourselves unable to tolerate difference, we might bring to mind Krishna's question: "Why this timidity, Arjuna, at a time of crisis?" What I see in the mirror I see with different eyes, my sight is based not only on an eye consciousness connected to the brain but also a cosmic eye-consciousness infused by and connected to the body as the field of existence itself. As we experience seeing ourselves in others and others in us, we deepen the knowledge of our actualization of interbeing—or readiness to surrender androcentrism to mysticism, where difference and sameness do not obstruct each other. Krishna assessed Arjuna as being ready to receive this teaching. Can you assess whether you are ready?

The Three Gunas or Qualities of Being: Differentiating Equanimity from Indifference

The Bhagavad Gita uses a three-part categorization scheme to understand the qualities and potentialities of our being. Called the three *gunas*, it is a type of categorization found in Hinduism, and it is used to assess the proportions of certain qualities thought to be present to differing degrees in everyone and everything. *Sattva* is the highest, *rajas* is in the middle, and *tamas* is the least favorable. Here is how they are explained in the Gita:

> Sattva is untainted,
> luminous, free from sorrow;
> binds by means of attachment
> to knowledge and joy.

> Rajas is marked by passion
> born of craving and attachment;
> it binds the embodied Self
> to never-ending activity.

> Tamas, ignorance-born,
> deludes all embodied beings;
> it binds them, Arjuna, by means of
> dullness, indolence, and sleep.[7]

I consider the three gunas as a tool for spiritual assessment. One can be primarily sattvic, but trauma can cause even a sattvic person to also experience tamas. One can be primarily tamasic yet work through the bindings and hindrances toward actualization. Rajas is always in play when new conditions and causes present themselves, especially as we contend with unexpected situations. As we aspire toward cleaning our mirror—a step we take in casting Indra's Net— to reflect the goodness of others, we can ask ourselves whether we are bringing sattva, rajas, tamas, or a combination of the three to what we are doing. And can we do so without self-congratulatory hubris and narcissism on one side? Without self-persecution and judgment of the other? Can we bring equanimity to however we assess ourselves as we work to de-intensify the I-sense? Doing so helps us move through the more limiting gunas—tamas and rajas—with more ease.

I mentioned in chapter 3 that I was sleeping in every class in my last year of college. I was in a profoundly tamasic frame of being: there I was, in an institution of higher learning, learning nothing and going nowhere until my professor confronted me and offered the idea to travel to Africa. His intervention was sattvic and inspired a sattvic frame within me, whereby I began to experience an appreciation for self-knowledge and embarked on a trip to the motherland. I do not recall any rajas in this transition, but I certainly lived in rajas when I was in 100 percent commissioned sales as a financial consultant. I then existed amid the seemingly never-ending activity of study, prospecting for clients, educating potential clients on their plan and product options, observing the markets daily and throughout the day, writing, publishing, and public speaking—all from the passion for the work, my clients and their financial well-being, and my own. This continuous, frenetic activity led to a form of rajas we know today as burnout. That burnout rajas, fortunately, led me to aspire to a more sattva-filled life.

Above, I encouraged bringing equanimity into our process of self-assessment so as to de-intensify the I-sense. Healthy equanimity can be a sign of sattvic energy flowing. Yet I want to offer the warning that there is also unhealthy equanimity, which carries a quality of avoidance and can promote spiritual bypassing. Let's look at both sides. First, the state of equanimity is a relief from the habitual unease with which we live our lives. To dwell equanimously in meditation for long periods of time is like being on the most restful vacation you've ever been on. It is not exciting, fun, or awe-inspiring, like when you see a beautiful mountain or lake for the first time, or when you're freshly away from the drudgery of work. It is more of a deep, slow settling into your own body and mind, noticing how much spaciousness, aliveness, and capacity for balance there is already present in yourself.

Contemplative spiritual aspirants often hear from their teachers that it is good to dwell equanimously. So, it is common that we come to place a high value on this experience, and we may even learn to return to it again and again as a way of transmuting desire. But there is a very thin line of emotional valence between equanimity and indifference, and it serves contemplatives well to study this line. Equanimity means not being easily swayed toward one side of an argument or situation and then dwelling polemically there. It involves the ability to see when one is attracted, attached, or stuck in a position, and why. True equanimity also involves the ability to step back from the stuck position in order to increase one's scope of observation, to have the optimum "position" to see and understand many perspectives—to be multiperspectival. This kind of dynamic equanimity takes ongoing practice. Indifference, by contrast, means not caring—not caring to know more, avoiding any investment in being affected, avoiding responsibility. When someone's "equanimity" carries this indifference, the people around them will sense a certain amount of aversion in that person. It is unempathetic and not compassionate toward suffering. There may be spiritual bypassing at play in the sense that the practitioner would rather use meditativeness to remain in their comfort zone than venture to learn about their own and others' suffering. It is a psychological defense. People experiencing and clinging to indifference do not dare to engage in interpathy. As noted in chapter 2, "interpathy" is a term coined by the pastoral theologian David Augsburger that means going beyond the feeling tone of empathy to the imaginative space of that person's social location, habits, worldviews, and life history. Venturing into interpathy will likely soften hardened positions on what is right or wrong, true or false. Although challenging such deeply felt views can be disconcerting, our collective survival depends, in part, on interpathy.

Knowing the difference between equanimity and indifference can inform how we understand the emotional valences of the three gunas. It can show the contemplative aspirant that what they thought was pure sattva (awakeness) might actually contain a heavy dose of rajas (attachment), or that their tamas (ignorance) has overlayed their sattva such that they are unable to respond freely to the suffering of others. The emotional valence of tamas is dull, that of rajas is compulsively excited, and that of sattva is non-anxiously present and aware. Through mindfulness of the body—its parts, sensations, and associated feelings—we can better determine what guna frames we are in.

In addition to explaining the three gunas, Krishna told Arjuna that there are two types of human beings: the transient (all of our bodies are impermanent) and the eternal (due to Self-actualization). In addition to these two types of human beings, there is the unchangeable Self that animates the universe and all in the universe—the one in all—and to love this one in all is the only thing one has to do after one knows what to love. Krishna told Arjuna to kill and also told him that all he needed to do was love the unchangeable Self, so what was he supposed to do? How did he make sense of these dueling commands? Krishna continued by introducing Arjuna to two broad categories of character traits: divine and demonic.

Divine includes

Courage

Purity

Determination in yoga practice

Generosity

Self-control

Nonviolence

Gentleness

Truthfulness

Integrity

Disengagement

Joyfulness in scripture study

Compassion for all

Modesty

Patience

Tranquility

Dignity

Kindness

Loving heart

Demonic includes

Hypocrisy

Insolence

Anger

Cruelty

Ignorance

Conceit

Krishna, having tested Arjuna by repeatedly commanding him to kill and Arjuna refusing, and having assessed him through the three gunas, determined that Arjuna possessed divine traits. Even in difficult and confusing circumstances, he was not drawn into cruelty. Yet, Krishna's talk of killing others continues! Krishna tells Arjuna that he himself has already killed people because they were the enemies of the divine. Because Krishna is the source within the source of all things, the death of these enemies was really caused by their ignorance, narcissism, rage, and addictions to desire, power, and wealth. The good news is they are impermanently dead to Self-actualization—there is always an opportunity for redemption. Now, Arjuna has a completely different understanding of what it means to kill others and what their death is like. He is not being called by Krishna to cause the physical death of others. They cause their own spiritual death and its physical counterpart means living an unactualized life. Think about this: Regardless of our worldview and religious or spiritual beliefs, we can be devoid of Self-actualization, living like zombies. Perhaps this possibility is evidenced by how popular zombie movies and television shows are—they convey a truth about our living-dead experience. Seeing zombies on-screen, we relate to the sense of emptiness, insatiability, ugliness, foulness, and abject disregard for the suffering of others.

Krishna gives Arjuna a mantra: OM TAT SAT. OM, according to the Gita, is a customary opening said before engaging in worship of many kinds. TAT is a word for the existence within existence—the Self, the Absolute—chanted before engaging in an act, unattached to the outcome. SAT means "goodness." OM TAT SAT, together, means "liberated mind" and is an expression of faithfulness.

Arjuna's Self-actualization deepens. I can imagine him utilizing this simple mantra to express all he has learned from Krishna up to this point in their dialogue. OM TAT SAT, OM TAT SAT—I know the good news of the Self within the self. Krishna knows Arjuna has divine attributes and has told him so, but Krishna is not done. He tells Arjuna more about renunciation—not just the importance of renouncing the outcome of his actions but also learning what action actually is. Krishna says action has five components: the body, the agent, the sense organs, the behavior, and divinity itself. What is the agent? The agent is the Self. The tamasic and rajasic person believes the agent is the person itself, attached to the I-sense, but the sattvic person knows the agent is the one free from the I-sense, free from attachment to results, the knowledge-known-knower.

And this is the crux of what differentiates Gandhi's understanding of the Gita as his "eternal mother" and guide to nonviolent action from the mundane understanding of killing. Gandhi wanted all Indians to live fully with dignity and self-determination, and in order for that to happen, British imperialism in India had to die. How? He had learned from the Gita, and his experiments with truth that he called *satyagraha*, that he could help the conditions for its death without attachment to the I-sense and therefore without a sense of separation. He wanted to withdraw the empire's nutrients—the Indian people and their resources—because it caused horrendous indignity, suffering, poverty, and death, but he was willing to do so patiently, collectively, and nonviolently because he was committed to understanding their coexistence with the British in the cosmic network. This is also why Gandhi's vision for postcolonial India was inclusive of all the country's religions and called for an end to "untouchability"—the status of the Dalits, the lowest caste.

Castes are maintained, in part, by mobbery. The Hindu chaplain who rightfully disrupted my thought patterns around my use of the word "caste" invited me into interpathy by also introducing me to a study called "Quantitative Methods for Investigating Anti-Hindu Disinformation," by the Rutgers Miller Center for Community Protection and Resilience.[8] As this study shows, there is Hinduphobia in the US and it is fueled by stereotypical tropes shared via hate groups throughout the world on social media. Sometimes the hate speech results in physical violence and death.

When mobbery is in play, a person is not only attached to their I-sense but has also surrendered their volition and agency to the mob—a kind of dangerous inverse of equanimous multiperspectivalism. In the state of mobbery, the agent can kill without regard for the consequences because they are relationally ill. By this I mean they are ignorant of the "strange fruit," to borrow the title of Abel Meeropol's anti-lynching anthem, famously recorded by Billie Holiday in 1939:

Pastoral scene of the gallant South
The bulgin' eyes and the twisted mouth
Scent of magnolias sweet and fresh
Then the sudden smell of burnin' flesh[9]

She was singing about the utter absurdity of lynching—hanging people to die from tree limbs created by God to bear flowers, leaves, and fruit. The sattvic person sees all beings as equal and does not lose sight of people's equality even when they are born into socially constructed castes. Rev. Hyde, the pastor of my youth, evinced sattvic awareness when he told me we were equally revered by God. But when he later tried to dissuade me from being gay, his guna, in my view, was tamas—deluded ignorance.

Deintensifying Caste Inclination:
Tonglen Meditation and Lojong Practice

One of the things that concerns me about mobbery is that it can be embodied by anyone regardless of their initially wholesome attitude or political persuasion. Many people are concerned about how deeply divided the United States really is. This concern is reasonable. For example, I know there was a time when the Democratic Party and the Republican Party were considered two sides of the same coin. This meant that to affiliate with one of these two mainstream parties was to have a currency that could be spent more or less anywhere in the country and even exchanged for cultural or economic currency outside the United States. Now, our political discourse suggests that each side has separate coins that represent different types of currency altogether. Don't fall for it. When I learned that US Rep. Adam Kinzinger, a Republican, was receiving hate mail because he spoke out against the coup attempt, I called him even though I am not a member of his party and even though he does not represent my district. I left a voicemail offering my pastoral support. According to some, there isn't just one United States. Some believe only an imposition of will, might, power, and strength can overcome this division. I worry that means we will see an escalation of mobbish impulses coming from each side to protect and preserve their power, but there is another way. We each need to ratchet down the intensity of our expectations on one another's level of political consciousness, resisting projecting a caste mentality onto others even when we suspect that is being done to us. Let me tell a story to convey what I mean.

In the mid-1980s, I lived in The Hague, a city in the Netherlands. I lived in a few different apartments while I was there, and for a time,

I rented a small room in the attic of an old white Dutch couple I will call the van der Blinks (not their real name). The van der Blinks told me, after I moved in, that they had secretly hidden Jewish people in that room when the Nazis occupied the Netherlands. Knowing that story from their history altered my relationship with this couple. First, they were no longer just old Dutch landlords—they were courageous, compassionate, justice-minded people who had put their very lives on the line to help others. Obviously, they were clever because they had not been caught in their "crime" *for* humanity. I had the utmost respect for them. The room became hallowed ground for me. Looking back, I lived in it as if I were in a Buddhist monastery, by walking and touching things carefully. I was very quiet in that room because I thought the space itself deserved the deepest respect.

The van der Blinks welcomed me into their home and were open to having meals with me. I felt they were treating me like I was part of their biological family—until, that is, several weeks or a month in. At that point, they began to ask me questions about my physical features. They had not befriended black people before meeting me, and there was an aspect of our connection that left me feeling as if I were an object in a shop of curiosities, maybe like the black South African Sarah Baartman felt when she was branded Hottentot Venus and exhibited in a freak show carnival.

I tell this story of my time with the van der Blinks in order to raise a question I think we must ask ourselves if survival through civility is our aim: Can we accept people when they don't know everything we think they should know? Should I have rejected the van der Blinks, who protected Jewish people at the risk of their own lives and who rented a room to me because their lack of prior exposure to black people resulted in questions that left me feeling awkward? We need to improve our ability to tolerate imperfection, and one way to do that is to accept our own many imperfections. In order to practice what I'm preaching, let me share that one of my "imperfections" is naivete (in case you haven't picked up on this already).

One reason I was able to accept the van der Blinks' imperfections was that, while in Europe, I went to one of the horrific places from which they had sheltered Jews. While living on a volunteer's monthly stipend of $75 (this is not a typo) after housing expenses, I saved enough money to visit Poland. I went to the Auschwitz-Birkenau concentration camp, where the Nazis tortured and incinerated over one million people during the Jewish holocaust. I believe it is important to note that although the overwhelming majority of people gassed to death were Jewish, non-Jews—including Poles, Russians, and white people from other countries, as well as disabled people, same-sex loving people, Jehovah's Witnesses, and others—were also killed. Everyone is at risk of some kind of death when genocide is taking place.

I struggle to articulate how I felt when I lived in the "hiding place" room, borrowing from Corrie ten Boom's book title. At times it was an overwhelming visceral sensation of internalizing horror. When I visited the Anne Frank House in Amsterdam, I cried uncontrollably. Similarly, when I visited a Mozambiquan refugee camp in Zimbabwe, I was stunned into silence. (Zimbabwe eventually resorted to mobbery, with disastrous economic effects.) Even as I write this, I notice the tension arising in me because I can't adequately describe the feelings. I remember that I was a sheltered and profoundly naive woman-child from Indiana, leaving the United States for the first time in 1984 for six weeks in Zimbabwe and again for two years in 1985 to live in the Netherlands. How do we breathe in this kind of suffering without disassembling our worldviews? I don't think we do. Breathing in suffering can be a sort of disassembling, just as I imagine Arjuna felt disassembled as he gazed into his oneness with Krishna in the middle of a battlefield. Maybe this is why we remain defended against com-passion, empathy, and interpathy—we know we will have to let go of our preconceived notions of what we thought was reality, and we don't know or trust that it will be replaced by anything we can tolerate and accept. Is the antidote not knowing? Not clinging?

———

The Tibetan Buddhist meditation practice of tonglen, sending and receiving, is a powerful practice used to lessen our defensiveness when we perceive another's suffering. It works as well to engage our moral imagination, maybe even our anthropological imagination, to see our-selves in others. This practice can enhance our capacity to be generous toward others, diminish the impulse to convince ourselves of our separation, and also calm ourselves when we initially don't know what to do. Tonglen practice is an act of radical non-discrimination because it engages the imagination with the notion that there is no meaningful difference between the sender and receiver, even though we use those words as conventions for communicating. Tonglen is a way to cast Indra's Net by shining the mirror, diamond, and pearl-like nature of our being because we are letting go of attachment to personality, identity, and ego formations in order to imagine meeting another's suffering and then act on it. In this undefended state, we have a greater capacity to reflect the reality of others.

I was introduced to tonglen and lojong, the incorporation of short phrases to cultivate compassion in daily life, by the Tibetan Buddhist nun Pema Chödrön when I attended one of her retreats in Oakland, California, in the early 2000s. At this retreat, Chödrön said she was working to understand Shantideva's wisdom chapter in his book *The*

Way of the Bodhisattva, a book that includes detailed instruction on tonglen. In short, tonglen meditation is about releasing our attachments to the project of personality making and sustaining, instead filling our imagination with images and thoughts of having the capacity and skill to attend to someone's suffering with radical generosity. This practice is a way to transform one's tamas (slothfulness) to sattva (non-anxious presence) by way of rajas (passion). Tonglen is cultivating Right Intention, moral imagination, generosity, and breathwork that reduces defensiveness. When we engage in a tonglen meditation, we bring to mind someone who or something that is suffering and we imagine attending to that suffering. In doing so, we are working to dissolve the psychological defenses that convince us we are separate from one another and that one person's suffering is over there, and my suffering is only in my discrete, encased body. By voluntarily engaging in this practice, one sacrifices their sense of psychic invulnerability by allowing the suffering of others to impact and inform them.

CONTEMPLATION
Tonglen Meditation to Release the Kleshas

In this explanation of tonglen, we prepare ourselves to release what is known in Buddhist psychology as *kleshas*. Kleshas are mentalities that can lead to unskillful or harmful behaviors.

Still your body, close your eyes, and imagine that you are breathing in purifying clouds. By imagining the clouds entering your nostrils and filling your lungs and entire body, you release yourself from the image of yourself and you imagine your "self" as space. The breathing need not be labored or extended. Take enough breaths to imagine your entire body is filled with clouds. Scan your body to detect any areas of tension and allow your body to relax as if you are a cloud.

In this relaxed and cloud-like state, free from the grip of the kleshas, bring to mind someone or a group of people you are in relationship with who is suffering. Hold that image in the area between your eyes that some call the third eye or mystical eye. Why there? That is the position of non-duality and non-discrimination. Softly hold the image there until your cloud-like sensation feels a connection, empathy, and even deeper still, interpathy. Having felt empathy or interpathy for the suffering, notice your breath without the expectation that your breath should be anything other than it is. What does your breathing tell you about how you're relating to the suffering?

Now, bring to mind how you understand the suffering. What might be the cause? What might be the release? What might be your role in the release? After contemplating this relational dynamic, return your attention to your breathing and imagine you are breathing in the suffering of your meditation object. If you notice some resistance, that's okay. It is normal to resist breathing in another's suffering. We are conditioned throughout our lifetimes to resist empathy, let alone interpathy, so accept that you too have been conditioned to be defended against doing so. Continue breathing as if your cloud-like nature has nullified the intensity of the kleshas. Trust in your cloud nature, your empty and flexible nature, and breathe in the suffering without holding your breath. Do not hold it, but exhale while imagining what relief would look like.

For example, if you know someone is hungry, breathe in the feeling of hunger and breathe out offering a meal. In this meditation, you are engaging the hippocampus, the part of the brain that imagines. If the suffering is shame, breathe it in and breathe out unconditional love. If the suffering is alienation, breathe it in and breathe out community. If the suffering is rage, breathe it in and breathe out peace. If the suffering is mobbery, breathe it in and breathe out individual autonomy, autonomy that means "self-directing freedom and moral independence."[10] In Buddhism, we call this being like an island.

After you imagine offering that which alleviates suffering, release your imagination from the clouds, from the images in the third eye, and return to "being on earth" but with a non-defended, imaginative, generous, and compassionate consciousness that reflects like mirrors, diamonds, and pearls. Make an effort to commit to living into your compassionate imagination.

Last, notice whether the suffering you imagined breathing in has become a part of your sense of self; if so, engage in self-compassion through lovingkindness meditation. In short, lovingkindness meditation involves keeping yourself in mind as you cultivate bodhicitta and direct the loving energy to yourself just long enough to feel it and just short enough to avoid the delusion of your specialness. I will return to detailed lovingkindness meditation instructions in chapter 7.

Tonglen meditation can be supported by the use of lojong slogans, of which there are fifty-nine. Here are three that I pulled randomly from Pema Chödrön's *Compassion Cards* deck.[11]

1. First, train in the preliminaries.

This slogan has to do with four daily reminders, including: remember that life is precious; remember that life ends; there is cause and effect; and self-absorption causes suffering.

13. Be grateful to everyone.

This slogan invites us to look into ourselves more deeply when someone provokes an uncomfortable feeling and reaction. We tend to say "thank you" to the person who pays us a compliment because we've been conditioned to appreciate how giving and receiving compliments nurtures relationships with agreeable people, but we are not conditioned to build relationships with people who annoy, anger, or just are not impressed with us. This lojong slogan supports teachings from the sages, like Jesus, who said that when someone violates you through violence or theft, do not retaliate. Wisdom also tells us there is a time and place for nurturing relationships with people who have hurt us, but in the meantime, in our hearts, we can appreciate if and how their injury to our ego has helped us see that we were actually clinging to our ego and that it is our ego that is injured, not our self.

26. Don't ponder others.

This slogan is about how we engage in "self-care" by not dwelling on the faults of others, thereby elevating our sense of self as superior. Self-care doesn't require minimizing others, so when we find ourselves returning over and over again to another's faults, notice and refrain, notice and refrain.

Can tonglen and lojong be used to ease the suffering of mobbery? I think they can. When I was in the Chicago high-rise with police helicopters above while protestors and rioters (not always one and the same) were having their say, I breathed in the ongoing suffering of the responses to George Floyd's torture and murder. In doing so, I felt the expressed anger and rage of the protestors and rioters without judgment. I knew the feelings (if not all the actions) were appropriate to the crime, and I trusted that the messages being conveyed would be heard. That message bears repeating: We are not a country that will tolerate police brutality when we see it. We belong to a family of nations that will not tolerate police brutality when we see it. What do we breathe out to ease the suffering of mobbery when we are in a crowd? Autonomy, beneficial influence, nurturing vibrancy, systemic resonance, and structural change.

Tonglen and lojong can be brought to bear to strengthen our prayer life. For example, what if we brought these practices to the Prayer of St. Francis? Rather than recalling and reciting it, we can bring breathing to it in this way:

CONTEMPLATION
Prayer of Saint Francis

Lord, make me an instrument of your peace.
   [imagine your whole countenance imbued with no impulse to harm, breathing in peace, breathing out peace]

Where there is hatred, let me bring love.
   [breathe in hatred, breathe out love]

Where there is offense, let me bring pardon.
   [breathe in the imagined offense, breathe out forgiveness]

Where there is discord, let me bring union.
   [breathe in the aggravation, breathe out harmony]

Where there is error, let me bring truth.
　　[breathe in the mistake, breathe out the correction]

Where there is doubt, let me bring faith.
　　[breathe in the disturbing confusion, breathe out confidence]

Where there is despair, let me bring hope.
　　[breathe in despondency, breathe out relief]

Where there is darkness, let me bring your light.
　　[breathe in ignorance, breathe out enlightenment]

Where there is sadness, let me bring joy.
　　[breathe in melancholy, breathe out enjoyment]

A F F I R M A T I O N
I can dwell in a state of goodness.

I know the deliciousness of enlightenment, spiritual kinship, interbeing, spiritual practice, compassion, and freedom from craving and clinging. I am ready to pursue the qualities of an awakening person. I aspire to dwell in a state of goodness. I can dwell in a state of goodness.

7

Knowing Your Place in the Cosmos

During the summer between my third and fourth year of college, I had a significant falling out with my mother. This came as a surprise because we were close—after my father's sudden death, I had made a decision to always be a "good girl." And, looking back, I see that my mother was my master teacher in the art of kinship and radical acceptance of difference. She was the first person, around 1982, to introduce me to a transsexual person, telling me that they deserved as much respect as anyone else. Now though, after a year of being a resident assistant in the dorm—a tumultuous year of student suicide attempts, terminal illness diagnoses, parties I was tasked to police, and witnessing the development of a secret sexual affair between two friends—I decided I had endured so much stress that I wanted to live in an apartment by myself to focus on my schoolwork and graduate "on time." My mother didn't approve of this decision because she didn't think I was mature enough to live on my own. In an attempt to make me change my mind and give herself peace of mind that I would be safe in a dorm, she unskillfully cut me off financially (in those days, even a financially struggling parent could contribute to public college tuition) and told me she would never visit me. I was shocked and devastated.

At the age of twenty-one, now a legal adult with all the rights and responsibilities pertaining to that rite of passage, after I recovered from that emotional blow, I thanked my mother for the support she had given me my entire life and told her it was actually my education, not hers, and that I should take on the responsibility for paying for it. Shortly before the school year began, I had two jobs to pay for my apartment. Lonely because my mother wasn't speaking to me, I decided to open the Bible for direction. I noted earlier in this book that reading the Bible and its many stories of violence eventually caused me to stop reading it, but before I stopped, at this juncture of individuating from my mother, I had a spiritual experience. The "voice of God," as I understood it, told me that my particular pursuit of an advertising career—the path I had chosen and was basing my studies around—was based on my own insecurities, greed, and ability to cleverly deceive others through creative copywriting. Although I knew that I could make a good living from it, something intervened as I read the Bible that day. The voice of God—which really meant my years in church and communion, the stories I heard about Jesus, and the woman screaming outside the church when no one but myself stood up for her and no one stood up for me—said that my career path should not be in advertising but in service.

This was the backdrop to my year of sleeping through classes. Although I had experienced a revelation about my purpose, I needed to integrate it into my sense of myself. That happened in part when my professor confronted me about sleeping in class, but I needed not just to know my purpose but to feel my fundamental belonging to the cosmos. Rev. Jerry Hyde telling me that I was as revered in the eyes of

God as he or anyone else had been an early seed of insight, but it was obscured by my youth and by the church's homophobia. Another one of the seeds that would awaken me to my cosmic belonging had already been planted. During my sophomore year living in the dormitory, one of my neighbors, Sherri, had a poster on her wall of the prose poem "Desiderata" by the American poet Max Ehrmann. It reads:

Desiderata

Go placidly amid the noise and the haste, and remember what peace there may be in silence. As far as possible, without surrender, be on good terms with all persons.

Speak your truth quietly and clearly; and listen to others, even to the dull and the ignorant; they too have their story.

Avoid loud and aggressive persons; they are vexatious to the spirit. If you compare yourself with others, you may become vain or bitter, for always there will be greater and lesser persons than yourself.

Enjoy your achievements as well as your plans. Keep interested in your own career, however humble; it is a real possession in the changing fortunes of time.

Exercise caution in your business affairs, for the world is full of trickery. But let this not blind you to what virtue there is; many persons strive for high ideals, and everywhere life is full of heroism.

Be yourself. Especially do not feign affection. Neither be cynical about love; for in the face of all aridity and disenchantment, it is as perennial as the grass.

Take kindly the counsel of the years, gracefully surrendering the things of youth.

Nurture strength of spirit to shield you in sudden misfortune. But do not distress yourself with dark imaginings. Many fears are born of fatigue and loneliness.

Beyond a wholesome discipline, be gentle with yourself. You are a child of the universe no less than the trees and the stars; you have a right to be here.

And whether or not it is clear to you, no doubt the universe is unfolding as it should. Therefore be at peace with God, whatever you conceive Him to be. And whatever your labors and aspirations, in the noisy confusion of life, keep peace in your soul. With all its sham, drudgery and broken dreams, it is still a beautiful world. Be cheerful. Strive to be happy.[1]

When I read "Desiderata" at nineteen or twenty years old, it was as if the secret to a happy life had been revealed to me for the first time. My father's death, our family's silence and experiences with racism and living on the economic margins, my experiences with homophobia — all seemed to disappear into the wisdom of this poster. What stood out to me the most was the phrase "You are a child of the universe no less than the trees and the stars; you have a right to be here." Why this line? In retrospect, it's obvious I didn't think I had the right to be anywhere. Sure, I was in college, but I didn't feel I had the right to be there. Growing up with a strict mother who told me repeatedly that I was an extension and expression of her, I didn't feel I had the right to find out who I was and be that person. Growing up as a descendant of Africa in a white flight neighborhood, later bused to white schools, I felt I had the constant responsibility to find myself beautiful. I'm thankful to have grown up in the era of black pride, which hit the scene when I was about eight years old. But even the constant reminders of black pride could not block out all the various forms of discrimination, violence, and deadly oppression I saw around me. Also, when I learned much later that I was attracted to women, I certainly didn't believe I had the right to love in that way.

So, to read that I had the same birthright as trees, stars, and other non-human entities was mind-blowing. Me, a child of the universe? I hadn't thought beyond the fifty miles I put between my mother's house in Indianapolis and my college campus, Ball State University—the Harvard University of Muncie (as David Letterman calls it). So, the thought I could belong to something so vast as the universe was amazing to me. I contemplated the universe as my parent, and this contemplation entered deep into the recesses of my mind—so deep, I often forgot to recall it when I needed it those many times in life when I felt I was not a part of the dynamic movement of life.

So, there I was in my last year of college, a child of the universe, endowed with the birthright to be just as the trees and stars, but sleeping soundly in every class. Thank goodness my professor cared enough about me to suggest I leave the country to see the world. Did I take his advice without question because of the influence "Desiderata" had on me? When I told my mother and aunt (the same one who in church told me not to attend to the person in distress) that I was going to Africa, their internalized racism scare tactics didn't penetrate me at all. Why was I, a person unwilling to go more than fifty miles away to college, suddenly able to plan a trip to the motherland? Maybe I had a sense of being a child of the universe after all. Before reading and being captivated by "Desiderata," there was the music of Earth, Wind, and Fire, the *Hair* soundtrack, and George Harrison's "My Sweet Lord." All my life, I heard about the concept of heaven, so I attribute all these things to the cultivation of a cosmic consciousness that would allow me to know, with conviction, that I am a child of the universe, and I believe my relationships are better for it.

How can we all begin to embrace our universal birthright as children of the universe? How can we know our place in a way that connects us to the cosmos as a parent without being too "woo-woo" about it?

In the previous chapter, we contemplated ways to improve our ability to be in community through understanding our deepening of compassion and improving our ethical obligations. In other chapters, we examined the stories of Yeshua's encounter with the Canaanite woman, the Parable of the Good Samaritan, the old woman serving mou mou to Te-shan, Angulimala joining the Buddha's community, Job's reintegration into his community, and Arjuna's quest to know Krishna. All these stories share one lesson in common—integration and reintegration into wholeness is the key to mutuality and healing. Wholeness acknowledges the interrelated reality of the cosmos. Cosmic existence in its entirety is really beyond our senses. Even though we have microscopes, telescopes, hearing devices, night vision technologies, satellites, drones, and other devices to help us perceive what the human senses cannot do alone, we still need the wise ones throughout time and tradition who have relied on faith and encouraged others to cultivate faith because we know we cannot know everything.

If we choose the ways of mutuality, we can live in community, being-with-unity, communitas. If we choose brutality, we are sure to live into destruction, being-with-disunity. In both cases, we are in the inescapable network. Trying to escape is foolish, sad, and harmful because it is impossible. Of course, there is mutuality and brutality in community because we don't all share the same insights, values, and relational skills. It is our job, if we are to call ourselves human beings, or beings trying to be human, in our short time on earth, to figure out how we are going to be, survive, and support one another to be, survive, and hopefully thrive. How will we not only reduce the bloody fingers and add to the fragrant flowers on our garlands but also help others to do the same? It will help to take some time to consider what it means to be part of the community in the cosmology, or cosmos, of our existence.

From the Scarcity Mindset to Cosmic Enoughness

Although our relatedness is ultimately with the entire cosmos, we can start with our simple human relationality. We are related to our parental unit(s), their parental unit(s), aunts, uncles, cousins, siblings, children, grandchildren, neighbors, and so on. We live where we live, located in our neighborhood, county, state, and country. This tends to be the limit of our sense of place-affiliation, but isn't it equally true that we live on a continent and a planet? Our planet, what we call Earth, is related to the star Sol, which we call the sun. Expanding our sense of connection even further, we are on the outskirts of the Milky Way galaxy, estimated by astrophysicists to be nearly fourteen billion years old. The Milky Way galaxy is "near" the Andromeda galaxy, relatively speaking, and so on.

At the time of writing (from fall 2021 to winter 2022), we are in an extraordinary time in history in terms of people having new views of our cosmic connectedness. Civilians are engaging in space travel! On July 11, 2021, Sir Richard Branson, the founder of Virgin Airlines, went to space. On July 20, 2021, the Amazon founder Jeff Bezos went to space. The geology professor, artist, poet, and African American woman Dr. Sian Proctor was one of four civilians on an all-civilian space flight on the Inspiration4 flight that took place on SpaceX Dragon on September 15, 2021. Dr. Proctor said:

> Oh, my goodness—opening the cupola and sliding my head up there and then seeing the entire sphere of our beautiful planet. And because I went up not only just as a scientist but

also as an artist and poet, to me, the earth became this kind of living painting, this moving, swirling ball. I just couldn't get enough. . . . I'm the fourth black female from the United States to fly to space, only four of us. And out of the four that have gone, only one person has gone multiple times. I really want to have that message out there that, you know, you can become a pilot. You can go to the stars—but not only for people of color and girls of color, but also for us what I call seasoned individuals. You know, I've been chasing space my entire life, and it took me 50-plus years to get here, but I made it.[2]

She could not have made it if she didn't already believe she was a child of the universe. It looks likely that more of us will get to see for ourselves what Dr. Proctor saw, but going to space need not be the only way we connect with our cosmic belonging. We can manifest our cosmic being by not allowing others to negatively define who and what we are. We can identify and renounce the ways we limit who and what we are by remembering our interdependence. We can do this with a mantra:

My body is part of a bigger body, the bigger body is part of me. Taking care of my body, I take care of the bigger body. Taking care of the bigger body, I take care of my body.

Our ability to separate ourselves from the bigger body, everything from our families to the galaxies, is only a figment of our imaginations—but our imaginings of separation can harden into views that feel so real they shut out whole aspects of reality. This is why we shut down to phenomena contrary to our preconceived and hardened views, why we feel we have to be right about everything to everyone all the time and shut out others who have differing views. One reason for our embrace of "alternative facts"—what we used to call lies and should return to calling lies—is the possession of a scarcity mentality. We don't think there is enough of what we need to go around, so we embrace lies that justify division and blame. The belief in scarcity fuels existential fear and paranoia that we will not survive unless we get our needs met first. My neighbor, who just like myself is of the nature to be vulnerable and fragile, becomes my nemesis, and in the fight to exist, the scarcity mentality can turn to an eat-or-be-eaten brutality. What kind of spiritual and ethical either-or choice is that? There is another option, one informed by an acceptance of ourselves as children of the universe who share the same cosmic sources of sustenance.

Knowing our place in the cosmos informs us of how small we really are, which, perhaps counterintuitively, can help us get out of the scarcity mentality. In the boundless scheme of life, we really don't amount to much, won't live that long, and can only consume a scintilla of nourishment. Much was consumed by countless beings before we existed, is consumed while we exist, and will be consumed after we are no longer in this present bodily form. When we ponder our relative smallness against the vastness of cosmic activity, we see that any sense of scarcity we carry is informed by the delusion that we are big enough to comprehend the world. What could actually be scarce in a cosmos that is full and diverse beyond our comprehension? Contemplating this insight can help us embrace the opposite of scarcity, which I think of as an "enough" mentality. This shift can lead to ease in collective body, collective mind, and collective spirit, promoting creativity to find and properly allocate resources, celebrate the normal rites of passage, and promote generosity and collaboration. Not eat or be eaten, but feed and be fed. As is prayed by hundreds of millions of people worldwide, "On earth as it is in heaven." We might start to make this prayer a reality by, for instance, agreeing that no one goes hungry because in the wholeness of our existence, there is enough.

We share the same bigger body, so it makes sense for us to begin acting as the relatives we actually are. How? Many spiritual paths invite us to accept the fact of our vulnerability and fragility, and through this acceptance, we can become humble. Through humility, we can accept that our egos convinced us that we were special, invulnerable, deserving, and so on, and that others were not. Then we can begin to put those self-delusions to the side and make space, through compassion, for others who are suffering. Through this Platinum Rule effect, discussed in detail in chapter 2, we can truly begin to adopt one another as kinfolk, unconditionally and without discrimination. As we do so, we can imagine that people close by and far away are our relatives and that we will relate to them as kinfolk in need and potentially kinfolk to rely on when we are in need.

One of the ways I have approached this understanding of spiritual kinship is through the Christian practice of communion, which I see as another form of wholeworking. In communion, at least in the United Methodist churches I grew up in, we were invited to the altar on the first Sunday of the month. Even though I was baptized as a child, I do not recall baptism being a prerequisite to receiving communion in the United Methodist Church. Everyone was free to approach the altar, kneel, and receive "the body and blood of Christ that was given to you." I ate the wafer, drank the grape juice, and kneeled in prayer with everyone at the altar. I believe communion is a ritual in cosmic belonging and place. When we are invited, without conditions and without discrimination, to gather together in humility to honor the sacred and that which is greater than us, the interpenetration of our collective vibrations can give us the physical sensation of oneness, kinship, or communitas. I have felt this over and over again, and I believe it is what El-Hajj Malik El-Shabazz (Malcolm X) felt in Mecca and what Thomas Merton felt in downtown Louisville. I believe you can experience this daily, almost anywhere, perhaps even among those who despise you. But this will only happen if you have the Right Intention toward kinship, which as we saw in chapter 3, means being curious about what is true, accepting the truth even when it feels painful, and not purposefully causing suffering.

The point about accepting the truth even when it feels painful is very important, as I don't want this teaching on cosmic belonging to become yet another rationale for spiritual bypassing. The truths of cosmic belonging and cosmic enoughness should not turn into justifications to ignore our particular relationships or to resist or deny observable facts all around us. To take cosmic belonging as a reason for contemptuousness toward the world is a grave misunderstanding, and one that is all too common among religious leaders.

Merton wrote in *Conjectures of a Guilty Bystander* in 1965:

The particular form taken by *contemptus mundi* [a fancy way of saying hatred for the world and worldliness] in this case was the assumption that theology had nothing to learn from the world and everything to teach the world. That theology was a store of static and eternal truths which were unaffected by any conceivable change in the world, so that if the world wanted to remain in touch with eternal truth it would do well to renounce all thought of changing.... New movements in thought, especially in science, which developed independently of the closed professional circle of theologians and jurists, were regarded with profound distrust as a secular threat, and were seen in a context of power struggle, not of love for truth. Thus, a traditionally spiritual and ascetic concept of liberation from the world, now used as a weapon for domination and suppression, become in fact a *contempt for truth*.[3]

Sound familiar? If religious leaders want to know why people aren't listening to them, they should contemplate whether there is any contemptus mundi operating in their theological consciousness. And if their contempt is being used to propagate lies, promote a scarcity mindset, and use fear to gather followers, that's all the worse.

In the end, being a child of the universe means we care about the universe as at least one of our life-giving and life-sustaining parents. Those with us in the universe are our kin, and thus we make our best efforts to take responsibility for the well-being of our family without care-prohibiting discrimination. Doing so means we don't create problems for others to solve, and we certainly refrain from intentionally harming our kin—but collectively, we're not there yet. Unfortunately, we are a species that still engages in war, genocide, and environmental racism; creates impoverishment; and so on. As children of the universe, we must make efforts to reverse our destructiveness.

Cherishing the Cosmos through Lovingkindness Meditation

Like most people these days, I live with many distractions—smart phone, laptop, TV, and all the comings and goings of a bustling neighborhood. For years, I thought that a general state of busy distractedness was the way I was supposed to live, but that changed when I first became deeply anxious. That happened on September 11, 2001. At that time, I was still working in the financial industry, and that day I was to fly home from a socially responsible investing conference in Tucson, Arizona. While at the airport, I received an uncharacteristically frantic call from my typically soft-spoken partner, imploring me to not board the plane—any plane. I began to notice that the lines at the ticket stands were long and that people were crowding around large-screen TVs in the bars. Joining them, I saw on screen what looked like a bombing of the World Trade Center. We began crowding around the screen and saw the horror as it was happening. Anxiety filled the space and filled my body. As it became evident that no one was flying out that day, I decided to take a long bus ride home to Oakland, California. By the time I arrived home, I was still anxious. Of course, the United States would retaliate. That is the way of much of the world, and the way we re-adjust positions, save face, maintain power, and seek protection. Within a month, the US president announced we would retaliate soon. We had been hit, we were hitting back, and my anxiety increased. I had a birthday approaching and I asked my friends if they could give me peace of mind as a birthday present. That is when a spiritual kin-to-be gave me the book *Touching Peace* by the Vietnamese Zen Buddhist monk Thich Nhat Hanh, a Vietnam war refugee. The first Buddhist meditation or visualization from his book is this:

Breathing in, I know I am breathing in.
Breathing out, I know I am breathing out.
Breathing in, I see myself as a flower.
Breathing out, I feel fresh.
Breathing in, I see myself as a mountain.
Breathing out, I feel solid.
Breathing in, I see myself as still water.
Breathing out, I reflect all that is.
Breathing in, I see myself as space.
Breathing out, I feel free.[4]

I immediately took to the calming effect of this brief meditation. Apparently, I was already geared toward seeing myself as other aspects of nature, but I didn't know why. Maybe it was being in the 4H club, where I learned to love cows and other farm animals. Maybe it was Frisky, Cubby, Jacques, and Chaggi—the dogs who were beloved members of my otherwise human family. Or maybe it was the twenty years of embedded "Desiderata." Whatever it was that geared me toward seeing myself as other aspects of nature, it took another twenty years before I realized the true power of this visualization—it is a contemplation of the mystic merging of mind, environment, and cosmos, and it supports acknowledging that our androcentrism blinds us to our cosmic substance. Once those blinders are off, we can deeply contemplate the interpenetration of existence without dread of the loss of our androcentrism. We can cherish ourselves, other people, non-human beings, and the whole seen and unseen world as the cosmos, which is a profound remedy for the anxiety of separation I was experiencing.

Those same twenty years that I was working toward a realization of the power in Nhat Hạnh's practice saw the prolonged, violent occupation of Afghanistan by the United States with seven thousand US casualties and an estimated 176,000 Afghan deaths. After all that, when the United States withdrew from Afghanistan, it only took several days before the Taliban recaptured the country. The Vietnam War similarly lasted almost twenty years. The Vietnam War gave rise to protest music by people who are now considered icons of the music world. I may have missed it, but I cannot say that the artists of the past two decades were focused on the tragedy of the Afghanistan War. We live in a country that goes to war as we go on with our daily lives. We are much less sensitive to the violence done in our names. The rhythm and blues singer Edwin Starr sang in 1970 that war, "Good God, y'all!" (a shock to the conscience) wasn't good for anything.

Whether musicians and artists are doing it or not, it is important that those of us who feel anxiety about war practice with our anxiety so its energy can be known and channeled constructively.

When I encountered Thich Nhat Hanh's breathing meditation, I was looking for relief from existential angst. I got not only that but also a new understanding of myself. I got access to the use of my imagination to see myself as non-human entities that are part of this world—a flower, mountain, water, and space! Space? Space! I didn't know it then, but I know now that I am part of space and space is part of me, and I believe this to be true of everyone. One need not leave the planet to experience space because we are already space. It's like these lines in the Tao Te Ching:

> The heavy is the root of the light.
> The unmoved is the source of all movement.
> Thus the Master travels all day
> Without leaving home . . .
> If you let yourself be blown to and fro,
> You lose touch with your root . . .
> A good traveler has no fixed plans . . .[5]

If we understand ourselves as having non-human elements, we can relate to non-human elements better. We have practiced this already, in the guided contemplation "Touching and Watering Your Seeds and Flowers" from the introduction to this book. Another way to improve our relationships with others, including ourselves, is through loving-kindness meditation, a wholeworking and cosmic-cherishing practice.

———

Much has been said and written about lovingkindness meditation (LKM). I want to focus on what I believe is the way LKM helps us return to the pristine and whole ego, which I think of as our consciousness before we make meaning of our unmet needs. It is a practice that promotes what I call Remarkable Relational Resilience. Remarkable Relational Resilience, in short, is the combined power of regular mindfulness practice, *vipassana* meditation and meditation retreats, lovingkindness practices, embodying interdependence, and sangha service. I learned this when I conducted research on the lives of Insight Meditation practitioners who are African-descended women-loving women. These practices, when developed as a lifestyle, help promote healthy relationality even when faced with various forms of discriminatory acts. Remarkable Relational Resilience, combined with a cosmic understanding of ourselves, can help de-intensify the impulse toward brutality and thus mobbery.

CONTEMPLATION
Lovingkindness Walking Meditation

LKM can be done in a seated or lying down posture or during walking or other types of movement. Since my focus throughout the book has been on refraining from the harm of mobbery, I will focus on walking and other forms of movement lovingkindness meditation (WLKM) as one way to do that. The "W" in WLKM stands for walking or non-walking forms of moving one's body from one place to another. Please adapt the practice to fit your abilities and circumstances. To engage in WLKM is a virtue because it is a practice in being dignified, disciplined, and positively inspiring.

One of the reasons why I advise at least sometimes practicing meditation while walking, or moving about in other ways, is because many of us spend a lot of time during the day in motion—getting to and from places and people, often in a hurry. The adrenaline rush of getting somewhere quickly takes our attention away from the motions involved in movement. When we don't have attention on our movements, there is likely to be a breach in the integrity between our beneficial thoughts, our capacity to bring those thoughts to bear, and our movement. If, in such a state, we find ourselves suddenly caught up in a conflict or the anger of a mob, we will be less able to differentiate ourselves and go our separate ways.

To begin a WLKM practice, dedicate fifteen minutes every morning to retraining yourself to move throughout life with love in your mind and heart. One word for "mind" in Sanskrit is *bodhi*, and one for "heart" is *citta*. WLKM practice is considered a *bodhicitta* practice—a practice to raise and integrate the awakened energies of mind and heart.

If you can stand, begin by standing with your feet about shoulder width apart and feel the solidity of being grounded in balance. If you are unable to stand, please adapt the instructions that follow to your seated or lying down position. You can emphasize feeling and perhaps moving the sides of your body, or you can remain still and coordinate the phrases with your breathing. Let your arms naturally fall to the sides of your body. It doesn't matter whether your palms face outward or align with your legs. Just allow yourself to stand in solidity and strength. Relax your shoulders. Feel your breathing expand your rib cage. Think about how the ability to stand, balance, and breathe (or whatever you are able to do, be it lying down or sitting) are acts that are often taken for granted, though they are not guaranteed abilities. Bring to mind a feeling of appreciation for your body. Bring a slight smile of gratitude to your face and feel what it feels like to have a slight smile on your face.

Notice how your body's postures influence how you feel. Feeling solid and appreciative, bring into your mind and heart the thought and feeling, "May I be free from suffering." Slightly lift your right leg to take a step, and as you bring your leg down and begin to lift your left foot, bring into your mind and heart the thought, "May everyone be free from suffering." Over the next few steps or moves, alternate: "May I be free from suffering" and "May everyone be free from suffering."

After taking a few steps or moves, pause. During this pause, reflect on your bodhicitta. What thoughts are in your mind? How do you feel in your heart space? Support integrity between head and heart. If you feel your bodhicitta is weak, continue your steps or moves, alternating between the same phrases, for the duration of your short WLKM. If you feel your bodhicitta strengthening, like there is no hindrance to you feeling bodhicitta for yourself, then take the next set of steps or moves with these phrases: "May my loved ones be free from suffering" as you step or move, "May their loved ones be free from suffering" as you take your next step or make your next move. Take a few sets of steps or moves, then pause. Notice your bodhicitta. If it feels weak, continue with this reflection, especially if you are not accustomed to thinking about the loved ones of those you love.

This bodhicitta practice involves extending your imagination beyond yourself and those you know. Being in Indra's Net doesn't require us to know everyone (that would be impossible), but the recognition of our place in the Net, in the cosmos, means we understand that our behavior affects those in close proximity as well as those far away through the vibrations of our actions, and vice versa. If, during the pause, you notice bodhicitta growing in capacity to hold and reflect the diamond, mirror, and pearl-like quality of others, the next set of steps can include this recitation: "May those who I've yet to love be free from suffering." Step or move. "May those I may never love be free from suffering." Step or move. This is a practice in casting Indra's Net.

This may seem paradoxical. How can we wish others to be free from suffering if we do not love them? If we have worked on the Platinum Rule, however—transcending the impulse to have our actions toward another predicated on how we feel about them—then we understand that our feelings about another do not supersede our desire and wish for their wellness. There is a hierarchy of moral and ethical commitments that we're choosing to move with. Like the Black Lives Matter activist, a modern-day Good Samaritan, who stopped to help the injured white man suffering from existential aggravation out of the crowd to avoid additional harm, we are prioritizing the well-being of others with these steps and moves.

Throughout our lives, we have accumulated a history of injuries and hurt. To move through life, we have had to do something with that pain. Depending on when the injuries occurred, especially if they occurred early in life when we had no ability to understand what happened, we, like countless others, may have misunderstood someone's capacity to harm as an innate quality of an entire group of people we think that person belongs to. That way of thinking gets reduced to a phrase such as, "All _____ people are _____." We generalize even further to justify attack: "All _____ people are _____ because they _____."

The next phrases are meant to counter this kind of conditioning about group-based perceptions. With the next set of steps, we say to ourselves, "May all _____ people be free from suffering. May I avoid being a cause for their suffering." Pause. Check your bodhicitta. Notice what comes up for you when you contemplate changing your thoughts and behaviors toward a group of people you have generalized, othered, despised, or had disregard for. This is the work of wholeworking and cosmic-cherishing. It will likely take more than one session of WLKM to notice and reverse the conditioning of a lifetime of injury, woundedness, and discrimination, but the time it takes to cultivate bodhicitta provides its own rewards. Keep at it.

This is a fifteen-minute daily practice with no guarantees, but it is a support for avoiding contributing to the dangers of mobbery. As you bring your WLKM to a close, bring to mind the phrase, "May all in Indra's Net be free from suffering, may I reflect back to others the goodness within themselves." Take a few sets of steps or moves. Pause. Check bodhicitta. Contemplate the reality of Indra's Net. Bring your palms together in front of your chest (prayer pose) and slowly bow. This slow bow is a ritual of humility, lowering your ego gratification to a psychic space that observes the moral and ethical commitments to lovingkindness and acknowledges our web of interconnected relations. In this bow, you position yourself to receive flower garlands from Indra's Net. Since this net is inescapable, let's be wise in how we choose to relate to all others.

WLKM can also be a way to prepare yourself to write your own WLKM *gathas*, should you so choose. "Gathas" are short sayings used in Buddhism to orient and concentrate the mind on wholesomeness while the body is in motion. I liken gatha practice to being poetry in motion. Here are a few WLKM gathas that I have written and that you can practice. Please adjust the language to fit your body and abilities:

Lifting my right leg or moving (if you cannot lift your leg) and breathing in—*I am aware I can move*

Lowering my right foot or moving and breathing out—*I am aware of my left leg's or body's support*

Lifting my left leg or moving and breathing in—*I am aware of the pressure on my upper leg or body's support*

Lowering my left foot or moving and breathing out—*I notice how my hips align*

Breathing in—*Moving with support*

Breathing out—*Pressure and alignment*

Breathing in—*Having cultivated walking or moving loving-kindness meditation, I walk or move in a crowd with the energy of peace*

Breathing out—*Part of the crowd, I notice the pacing of the crowd*

Breathing in—*Energy of peace*

Breathing out—*Noticing pacing*

Breathing in—*Lifting my right leg or moving, I notice whether my own pacing is faster*

Breathing out—*Lowering my right foot or moving, I notice the difficulty in noticing my left leg or body*

Breathing in—*Faster pace, loss of attention*

Breathing out—*Lifting my left leg or moving, I notice agitation*

Breathing in—*Lowering my left foot or moving, I notice my dislocation*

Breathing out—*Agitation, dislocation*

Breathing in—*Lifting my right leg or moving, then my left leg or moving, I notice I'm moving too fast to notice the in-between movements*

Breathing out—*Losing the ability to notice, I recall my vow of peacefulness*

Breathing in—*Moving too fast, recalling vow*

Breathing out—*Remembering vow, I stop*

Breathing in—*Stopping, I renounce the crowd's hysteria*

Breathing out—*Remembering, renouncing*

Breathing in—*Renouncing violence, I turn my body in another direction*

Breathing out—*No violence, noticing those around me*

Breathing in—*Going against the stream of hysteria, I invite others to join me*

Breathing out—*Departing, departing*

Breathing in, breathing out—*Feeling gratitude for the path of blamelessness*

We cannot really feel love unless we can really absorb the vibrational quality of empathy. Mindfulness meditations, such as WLKM and gathas that touch your mind and heart, are ways to get in touch with your feelings and the feelings of others. It takes commitment to cultivate wholeness in community, being-with-unity, communitas, and the cosmos. In order to live this way, it is helpful to understand who and what we are and have faith in who and what we can become for one another. When we better understand suffering and its causes, we learn the path of selflessness and generosity toward others. When we value and cultivate compassion, empathy, and interpathy, and thus commit to the well-being of others in our communities (knowing it will ripple out to communities beyond), we begin to better understand that we are living in an existence beyond our bodies, the community, even the planet.

AFFIRMATION

*I cultivate the determination to awaken
and live for the welfare of others.*

As you cultivate compassion, there may be people who used to know you as an aggressive person and will not like the person you're becoming. If they are about violence, they may use violence to coerce you back into their violent worldview and community. Though they destroy things, ultimately they destroy themselves until, like you, they are shown another way. Polish your mirror, shine your jewels, buff your pearl-like qualities every day, as simply as if you were taking a drink of water. The quality of your life, in a world grown increasingly violent, depends on daily self-nurturance and self-compassion. Shine and reflect for the welfare of all others. I cultivate the determination to awaken and live for the welfare of others.

———————————————————

8

Letters from a Chicago Condo

*To Rev. Dr. Martin Luther King Jr.
and to My Buddhist Kin*

Dear Rev. Dr. Martin Luther King Jr.,

The title of this book is inspired by the embedded Eastern theology of your famous quote,

> I am cognizant of the interrelatedness of all communities and states. I cannot sit idly by in Atlanta and not be concerned about what happens in Birmingham. Injustice anywhere is a threat to justice everywhere. We are caught in an inescapable network of mutuality, tied in a single garment of destiny. Whatever affects one directly, affects all indirectly.[1]

I started the book, however, with a different quote, one from your essay "The Three Dimensions of a Complete Life," because I wanted to begin at the point of our collective economic pain. I wanted to begin with the feeling of being impotent in the global marketplace, a feeling of insignificance in the national and global marketplaces, the frustration of being caught between industry and inferiority that has been exploited before in America and is being exploited again, turning us irrationally against one another in a madness the likes of which even you did not see—or did you? Rev. Dr. King, I am writing to invoke your black Christian-Gandhian satyagraha spirit for our encouragement, enlightenment, and collective survival.

I am a black Buddhist leader born in 1961, just a few years before you wrote your letter from a Birmingham, Alabama, jail cell. I am writing you this letter even though you were assassinated in 1968. I think it is strange for me to write a letter to someone who has died, but this isn't the first time I've tried to be in dialogue with you since your death. The last time was in 2016 in Atlanta, Georgia, when I visited a center for nonviolence named after you there. This time, I am communicating with your enduring spirit for a different reason.

I've read your letter many times over my lifetime, even though you did not address it to Buddhists but to Christian pastors who criticized your involvement in loving civil disobedience to transform our racist society. Reading your letter this time inspired me to write this letter because, nearly fifty years after the arguments you had with Christian leaders, I find myself having similar arguments with Buddhist leaders. Many Buddhist leaders criticize anti-racist Buddhists for not acting how they think Buddhists should act. I am confounded, as you were, by how people who espouse love and compassion will sit by (and in our case literally sit, in meditation) while so many black people are incarcerated or caught up in the criminal justice system, remain stuck in poverty, are still subject to police brutality, and so on.

That's one reason I'm writing you this letter. Another reason is to describe to you the world as it stands today, in the hope of seeing it more through your wise, compassionate, and courageous eyes. I am happy to let you know that some of your dreams have been fulfilled. I grew up with white children as schoolmates. My black daughter had white playmates, including our Mormon neighbor's children. And, in 2020, after an unarmed black man named George Floyd was tortured and murdered in Minneapolis by a police officer who choked him with his knee for over nine minutes, in broad daylight, in front of several witnesses pleading for mercy and capturing the atrocity on camera, scores of thoroughly integrated activist coalitions took to the streets around the country and the world in a way that would have made you cry tears of joy. So, on the one hand, much progress has been made. On the other hand, there's still so much to do.

I perceive that American Buddhists are ethically well-positioned to be activists, though many argue that it is not Buddhist to be social change activists. I wonder if anything in your letter to Christian pastors can be instructive for us Buddhists? Not having suffered the way you did—I've never been stabbed, repeatedly threatened, had my family threatened, been imprisoned, or had someone try to assassinate me—I wonder if I'm even worthy to correspond with you, but I'm willing.

———

In your letter, you begin by saying that you don't spend a lot of time answering criticisms, but because you believe these Christian pastors are of goodwill, you will answer their concerns. I believe most Buddhist leaders are of goodwill because I am familiar with our core Buddhist aspirations—to understand the nature of suffering and walk the path of relief from suffering. We also say that ignorance, hatred, and greed are at the root of all transgressions and that the relief of suffering includes the transformation of ignorance into wisdom, hatred into love and compassion, and greed into generosity. We say we believe in enlightenment, and though I don't consider myself an enlightened person, I have benefited greatly from Buddhism. Because

I have benefited, I believe others have too. But what am I to do with this belief when I find so few of my fellow Buddhists standing together on behalf of social justice? Before I continue with that question, let me tell you more about what has happened in America and in the world since you were so tragically taken from us.

I'm imagining you, the most prominent leader of a freedom movement, in that Birmingham jail cell in 1963. I'm in a Chicago condo in 2022 as I write this letter, about as free as you and our abolitionist and liberationist ancestors fought for me to be. My freedom is thanks in large part to: enslaved people's rebellions, a diverse coalition of abolitionists, countless hidden unsung heroes, the activism of the National Association for the Advancement of Colored People (NAACP), the National Lawyers Guild, the Southern Christian Leadership Conference, the US Supreme Court's decision to desegregate schools in *Brown v. Board of Education*, the civil rights movement (including the Student Nonviolent Coordinating Committee and the Black Panther Party), Congress passing the Voting Rights Act, and the jurisprudence of Thurgood Marshall (who, you'll be glad to hear, served on the Supreme Court until his retirement in 1991). Just this year, another important step has been taken: the first black woman, Judge Ketanji Brown Jackson, was confirmed to be the next Supreme Court justice (albeit by a deeply ideologically divided Senate). But the George Floyd Act of 2021, to reform policing, was not passed—and this is just one of many examples of racial prejudice, not to mention other kinds of prejudice and structural inequality, that persist in our society. Even though black and white children can be educated together, and society is a lot less segregated by law than it was when you were here, the horrible delusion of white existential aggravation has reared its ugly head in a way this nation hasn't seen since Reconstruction—and I'm not exaggerating! Let me explain . . .

Would you believe we had a two-term black president? His name is Barack Obama, he served as president from 2009 to 2017, and I am confident you, with your own political astuteness and sophistication, would have approved of his presidency. Unfortunately, his eight years in office—a black man with a black wife and their black children living in the White House, doggedly pushing for universal health care and other pro-social flourishing policies—scared the you-know-what out of many Americans. A man who would become President Obama's main public nemesis when Obama was a candidate joined the ranks of those who stirred up that fear and channeled it in the direction of conspiracy theories, xenophobia, and hatred. This hatred was expressed as racism, of course, but also as Islamophobia and aggressive nationalism. Many Americans became convinced that our forty-fourth president, our first black president, was not born in the United States and was Muslim. (He was born in Hawaii and is Christian.) Anti-black and anti-Muslim sentiments were subsumed into a political slogan, "Make America Great Again," which in truth is anti-American in its disdain for the country's complex history and pluralistic present. Obama's main public nemesis, who had never held political office of any kind before, became the forty-fifth president. His name is Donald J. Trump. The United States thus showed itself to be a teeter-totter of starkly opposing national values.

Shortly after the forty-fifth president of the United States took office, white supremacists and white nationalists, without the cover of white KKK hoods, brazenly began recruiting white people on college campuses. These attempts were met with resistance by people dressed in black called anti-fascists, or Antifa for short. There was a violent clash at the University of California, Berkeley. Right—Cal, home of the free speech movement! The white supremacists tried to make the campus a place of free hate speech rather than a bastion of free peace speech.

Through this and many similar clashes, we have entered an era of re-symbolizing—on the one hand, removing and prohibiting symbols of hatred like the Confederate flag; on the other, removing and prohibiting teachings about racism or gay identity, especially in schools.

In the midst of this tense situation, I believe Buddhists have some-thing to offer—we teach equality; we say we believe the substance of who we are, and are not, is equal, non-dual, empty, impermanent; we say that race is a construct and that identity politics is fraught with suffering. I think that these and other Buddhist teachings are well-suited for application toward social justice activism. Yet only a minority of us put our necks out, while the rest of us, if we say anything at all, criticize Buddhist activists like your fellow pastors criticized you. Should Buddhist activists keep doing what you did—that is, attempting to justify our positions to Buddhist leaders be-cause we believe they are of goodwill?

Dr. King, I think we Western Buddhists have the problem of conflict avoidance. In your letter, you explain to pastors that "nonvio-lent direct action seeks to create such a crisis and foster such a tension that a community which has constantly refused to negotiate is forced to confront the issue."[2] I can assure you that this is not the conventional way of dharma practitioners in the West. The resistance to tension is so thick sometimes you need a chainsaw to cut through it. I suspect this is the main reason why people of color (POC) leave predominantly white sanghas (Buddhist communities) and form POC sanghas. Although I find the need for ease that leads to racial affinity groups understandable, I worry about the possibility of perpetual separation of affinity sanghas. I wonder if there can be a time for ease and a time for tension in all of our sanghas because, to your point, without tension and crisis there is little reason for stuck parties to negotiate. Buddhists, adhering only to attention on the present moment, yet spiritually bypassing the moment when we find it full of tension, do not collectively engage our imagination toward the creation of havens for the prevention of harm. I guess that's why we have to talk to each other like you talked to the Christian pastors who asked you to get back in line and be satisfied with a vague incrementalism. It is time for Buddhist leaders to get out of line.

Since your death, one of your sayings—"Injustice anywhere is a threat to justice everywhere"—has been repeated in many contexts and received broad acclaim, and it resonates with Buddhist teachings on interdependence. But right now, I don't think people really believe it or are willing to address it.

In February 2017, after President Trump, though no model for the Christian life, became the chief torch bearer of Christian nationalism and Islamophobia, he announced he would sign a religious freedom executive order. Rev. King, thinking about the many times you called us to do something, I crafted, posted, and sent a petition called "Embrace Others Now." It reads:

Dear President Trump,

We are people of faith writing to ask that you trust the strength of the US Constitution, as we do, and not issue an executive order on religious freedom.

The US Constitution, this country's most revered and respected organizing document, says in the First Amendment that "Congress shall make no law respecting an establishment of religion, or prohibiting the free exercise thereof; or abridging the freedom of speech, or of the press; or the right of the people peaceably to assemble, and to petition the government for a redress of grievances." We are a stronger nation for the fact that neither Congress nor any other governmental branch has established a religion, but we also understand that many citizens wonder whether the government has or will prohibit the free exercise of our religions. We share that same concern.

Initial research into the impact of religious freedom laws reveals that legislative attempts to protect religious freedoms may actually undermine the practice of historic Judeo-Christian ethical values. One study, a survey of chaplains and pastoral counselors in Mississippi, Alabama, Florida, Georgia, Tennessee, North Carolina, and South Carolina, co-sponsored by the American Association of Pastoral Counselors Southeast Coordinating Committee, shows that a significant number of those surveyed believe that "restore religious freedom" laws have negatively impacted the practice of compassion and empathy in their states. We feel confident that it is not your intention through executive order to undermine the heart of Christian values. Nevertheless, the undersigned people of faith see the undermining of Christian values of love, compassion, and empathy (values shared by other religions) as a distinctly real possibility.

President Trump, this world has seen the horrors of so-called religious freedoms gone unchecked. Husbands were permitted to rape their wives on religious freedom grounds. White people were permitted to enslave black people on religious freedom grounds. Christian Nazis were encouraged to exterminate Jehovah's Witnesses, gay people, mentally ill people, people with intellectual developmental issues, and Jewish people all on religious freedom grounds. Babies and children have been denied life-saving medical care on religious freedom grounds. Girls have been kidnapped, raped, forcibly converted, and sold into slavery on religious freedom grounds. No one is really safe from unchecked religious freedom.

The US Constitution's Fourteenth Amendment provides protection from the pandemonium of religious freedom through its equal protection clause. The amendment reads "No state shall make or enforce any law which shall abridge the privileges or immunities of citizens of the United States; nor shall any state deprive any person of life, liberty, or property, without due process of law; nor deny to any person within its jurisdiction the equal protection of the laws." The Fourteenth Amendment helps our nation move beyond our segregationist past, and it is a living protection for all citizens against the government's intrusion into our religious freedom.

We believe the First and Fourteenth Amendments, in tandem, work well to protect Americans from the imposition of religion and religious oppression. An executive order to "restore religious freedom" is unnecessary and potentially harmful, running the risk of undermining the heart of Christian values. We ask that you refrain from issuing a religious freedom executive order.

I shared this petition widely using petition-sharing software, social media posts, and by sending some six hundred emails. Only eighty-eight people signed the petition. I am confident that hundreds of Buddhist leaders and practitioners saw the petition, and I feel disappointed that so few chose to make the small effort to sign their names to it, not to mention supporting it in other ways. I shared the fact of the low response when I was a presenter on a womanist theology panel at the American Academy of Religion because I was not ashamed the petition was largely ignored, but I remained very concerned that the United States was headed for trouble. The religious freedom executive order had real policy consequences, especially for members of the LGBTQ community in healthcare contexts who were denied treatment based on the religious beliefs of healthcare workers.

————

Rev. Dr. King, we are living in a worldwide pandemic caused by a virus called COVID-19. Shortly after the pandemic hit the United States—and hit it hard, especially in New York City—when word spread that mostly black and brown people, those with underlying health conditions, and those who were elderly were most at risk of death, the president, and some Republican governors who sought to appease him rather than follow public health guidelines, eased public health protocols. One of those measures was to wear a mask over your mouth and nose. Would you believe wearing a mask became a sign of whose political party you supported? Rather than form a unified front to sacrifice together and minimize losses to this disease, much of the country, under Trump's sway, quickly entered into xenophobia against "Asian-looking people." We witnessed a descent into paranoia, blame, and antagonism. Now, nearly three years into this pandemic, an estimated 300 people in the United States are dying of the virus *every day*—and this is a far lower number than during the peak. An overwhelming number of them refused to receive the vaccines that were created in a concerted effort of scientific efficiency. (The president supported creating the vaccines while also questioning science and scientists in various ways, sending mixed signals to his followers. When he contracted COVID-19, he received medical treatment based in science.) Millions of people who survived having COVID-19 will live with chronic ailments related to what's called "long COVID." The United States has surpassed one million deaths and the world has seen over six million. These numbers are certain to rise if we don't privilege mutuality over brutality.

If your dream had been fully realized, our national and state leaders would have made specific moves to protect those most vulnerable to COVID-19, but that was not the case. Businesses were closed but were allowed to prematurely open again, and I am sure that the thought that healthy white people would not die of COVID-19 influenced this decision. Although we now have several effective vaccines, only 15 percent of people in low-income countries have even begun to be vaccinated, and momentum is ebbing from the movement to share vaccines equitably around the globe. American contributions to the World Health Organization were defunded by President Trump in the early days of the pandemic, and he also did everything he could to publicly undermine public health officials on his team, including the Centers for Disease Control and Prevention (CDC). Why? Ostensibly to protect the economy. His reputation, in focus because a presidential election was looming, rested on the nation's economic growth. He preferred to deny the existence of the virus or, when that didn't work, to blame it on the Chinese, or to accuse his political opponents of overreacting—anything other than to truthfully face the situation. So many people died on his watch and are dying still because of the refusal to radically contain the spread. We are going to live with COVID-19, its variants and subvariants, for years. It is heartbreaking.

The virus was declared discovered in China on December 31, 2019, and was declared present in the United States on January 21, 2020. In November 2020, a presidential election was held, and it was won by Joseph R. Biden Jr., the man who had served as Obama's vice president. Biden was installed as president on January 20, 2021, but not in a way you would expect. Biden's vice president is Kamala Harris, who is the first woman and the first person of color to hold the position. Those "colors" are "brown" for her Indian mother and "black" for her Jamaican father. Her parents were brilliant: her mother was a cancer researcher with a PhD from the University of California, Berkeley, and her father a PhD economics professor at Stanford University. Does this not blow your mind? Harris, of course, is accomplished in her own right as a former defense attorney turned California state attorney, then California senator, and now vice president. Now brace yourself for the real shocker. Two weeks before Biden was inaugurated, there was a violent coup attempt wherein US citizens forcibly entered the Capitol. They threatened elected officials, including President Trump's vice president, Mike Pence, who was escorted out, with others, through a secret passageway.

With Harris as vice president and other people of color in various posts—including Debra Anne Haaland, a Laguna Pueblo tribe member and the first Native American to be a White House cabinet secretary, as the secretary of the interior—the Biden administration is perhaps even more of a nightmare to those suffering from white existential angst than Obama's administration. The realization of aspects of your dream has thus manifested as nightmares for those who support racial segregation (in their actions if not their words)—a group that continues to hold significant power in this country. I wonder if you knew that would happen.

In the months between the 2020 election and Biden's inauguration, the teeter-totter of starkly opposing national values was poised in a fraught, liminal space. It had been a hotly contested election and President Trump trumpeted the "big lie" that it had been stolen from him and therefore he would refuse to leave office. On January 6, history was made. We had a coup attempt! The forty-fifth president encouraged his followers to come to Washington, DC, mob the Capitol, and try to prevent the certification of the election of the forty-sixth president. It was the big mobbery. The United States can no longer claim an unblemished record of peaceful transfer of power. Can you believe what I'm telling you about your beloved United States?

President Trump underwent two presidential impeachments in his one term. One of those impeachments had to do with asking the president of Ukraine to do him a favor in 2019. Trump blocked payment of a $400 million military aid package and all but stated that a Ukrainian investigation into Joseph Biden's son's business dealings in Ukraine was the precondition for the aid to be released. The Senate did not hold Trump accountable even though the facts were never seriously in question. Russia invaded Ukraine in a brutal war beginning in February 2022, which continues as of this writing. Rev. King, your dream included a de-escalation of US militarism, aggression, and imperialism. I hope we don't forget that, but how can we remember if many of us don't value facts and truth? Tens of millions of Americans still deny that Trump lost the last election and still support him for re-election! Our situation is dangerous, and as you said about our inescapable network of mutuality, injustice anywhere is a threat to justice everywhere. I see that. You died because of our violence, our fear of love, our fear of equality, and the fear that we'd have to play on a level field—no slavery, no Jim Crow, no "a woman's place is in the home," no imperialism, no colonialism.

———

I'm sure you can tell, from all I've just written, that America still faces a host of profound social and political challenges. Many courageous people are attempting to face them squarely. I believe you would be proud of the Christian pastors Revs. William Barber and Liz Theoharis, who lead the national Poor People's Campaign, continuing your work to this day. Noting that these are Christian leaders, not Buddhist ones, returns me to my question about my fellow Buddhists. What is missing from American Buddhism that prevents it from replicating the strong connection between religious faith and activism evident in the lives of Christians such as yourself and Revs. Barber and Theoharis?

In your letter, you talk about being inspired by Christian activists who came before you. In Buddhism, we would call this a lineage. But very few of the iconic figures in our lineages—our Buddha or Buddhas, Anandas or Sariputtas, nor even our deities or bodhisattvas—are regarded as civil rights activists or anti-racists. What should we Buddhists do when we can't place ourselves in a lineage of Buddhist human rights or civil rights activists? You also make references to the Christian theologians Reinhold Niebuhr and Paul Tillich. Fortunately, American Buddhism does have a growing number of black Buddhist thinkers and writers producing dharma talks, articles, and books that offer Buddhist perspectives on how to transform society. (Some of the more well-known such figures include the Insight teacher Ruth King, the Zen priest Zenju Earthlyn Manuel, the Triratna leader Vimalasara Mason-John, the Tibetan Buddhist Lama Rod Owens, the radical dharma practitioner and scholar Jasmine Syedullah, the scholars Rima Vesely-Flad and Jan Willis, and the Zen priest Rev. angel Kyodo williams—and there are many others.) Yet there remains much criticism.

In your letter, you anticipate criticisms: "Why be disruptive?" "Be patient." And so on. I think you answer these questions and criticisms brilliantly, but what I think is most important is how you highlight the history and continuation of white people brutalizing black people. I can't help but think about how society tried to pit you and El-

Hajj Malik El-Shabazz against each other, but you both understood that white existential paranoia is brutal. As I already told you, white people are still invited to be brutal toward black people. Centuries of ignorance about the fundamental equality of races led various white societies to self-aggrandizement as world conquerors, colonizing vast regions of the Earth, enslaving people and transporting them to other lands, the United States included. Such ignorance will not completely abate overnight or over a year, a decade, or even centuries. We have to keep dreaming, imagining we can advance civilization. I'm reminded of a quote attributed to your spiritual ancestor and spiritual mentor Mohandas Gandhi. When asked, "What do you think of Western civilization?" Gandhi replied, "That would be a good idea." Brilliant! Western civilization continues to be a good idea and a necessary project. How should we proceed?

In our nation where the appetite for authoritarianism is increasing, I am reflecting, Rev. Dr. King, on the fact that your spiritual movement was political and your political movement was spiritual. I believe you want us to continue engaging our politicians. In November 2020, as I was reflecting on the possibilities a new administration could usher in, I wrote this unpublished op-ed piece:

Nation, Heal Thyself

We are entering the first holiday season of this coronavirus pandemic, and we are entering it sick and suffering. We are sick with COVID-19 and other illnesses and growing more vulnerable every day. President-elect Joe Biden said that in order to heal our divided nation, we have to "lower the temperature" of our rage, see each other as fellow citizens, and follow public health directives. His prescription is not new, but his place in the political order is. Place matters, empathy matters, and so does psychological acumen. To avoid saying the same things over and over again, resulting in a worsening situation, our leaders need to understand that our greatest suffering has not come from the disease but rather from the violently intense quality of our national collective consciousness. It feels like we stand at the borderline of breakdown. Healing will come if those at the top can facilitate a national dialogue that is dialectical in nature.

Such a dialogue begins with the recognition that our national division has reached a dangerous point of diametrical opposition. We have become a this or a that, black or white, with me or against me, Republican or Democrat. "Or" signals two significantly limited and oppositional perspectives. Despite these limitations—which include the limitation of being defined only in opposition to each other—both positions contain validity. Those at the top will have to learn how to hold both sides with neutrality. They will have to be a this and a that, black and white, with me and with them. "And" signals nondualistic possibilities. Democratic leaders will have to find the Republican inside. Biden has to find the black female within, Harris the white male within, they both have to find the gay person within—and so on. If they do so, together they can better hold the complexities of our sick and suffering nation while paving the path of wellness. But I agree with President-elect Biden that first, the temperature of our collective rage has to be reduced to a simmer.

One way to help lower the temperature of rage is for government to be as transparent as possible. Our national psyche now exists largely on a spectrum from suspicion to paranoia. We have become suspicious to the point of being truly afraid of each other. This fear leads us to lean into the posture of preemptively striking each other—sometimes literally. Governmental transparency will be an effective way to work through the suspicion-paranoia spectrum and thus reduce the tendency toward violent rebellion. We also have to learn how to soothe our aggression.

Mindful breathing has been proven effective in reducing tension in the mind and body. Mindful breathing is a simple exercise that brings one's mental attention to the sensations of the breath—the tingling around the nostrils, for example. The more mindful breathing is practiced, the greater the resource the practice becomes when someone is agitated and recognizes their agitation in the moment. The ability to recognize one's agitation in the moment improves when one practices mindfulness of bodily sensations. Practicing mindfulness of bodily sensations also improves our ability to utilize this resource when we realize our agitation could potentially lead to violating (through speech or physical touch) another's boundary. Those at the top of government have a new responsibility—to model mindfulness so as to reduce triggering the traumas that have occurred in our sick and suffering nation.

Last, President-elect Biden needs to recognize that, for all of his desire to heal the nation, he cannot heal this nation alone. We must want to heal ourselves—and we can. Many people surrender to what heals only when the desperation of sickness and suffering becomes unbearable. We are at the tipping point. When more of us realize that our decisions to flout public health directives are in the causal chain that leads to our medical teams and hospitals literally breaking down, we will possess more clarity about how this pandemic affects us all.

The United States needs a secular Billy Graham–like figure to be a modern-day ethical torchbearer. Such a person would skillfully facilitate dialectical dialogue by embodying the neutrality necessary to address our national polarization, help each side see its own and the other's complexities, remind us to breathe, and coach us to wellness. The rest of us need to notice our own polarized minds, bring mindfulness to our breathing and bodies, examine the facts in the face of conspiracy theories, and commit to the principle of one nation under our Higher Power. This is the season of gratitude and generosity. The holiday season could not be at a better time.

Dr. King, even though the Embrace Others Now petition was not signed by many people, even though my op-ed piece was not published, and even though Representative Adam Kinzinger did not call me back when I called him to offer my pastoral support (I didn't ask him to), I take heart in your determination to stay spiritually and politically engaged to the end. I hope that publications like Buddhist Justice Reporter can inspire people of goodwill to do the good that is needed. I want to sincerely thank you for your example. And I hope that, in trying to follow your example, I am also setting an example for other Buddhist leaders, and spiritual leaders of all kinds, to try and alleviate suffering by engaging in political communication and activism.

What do you think it will take in these "post-truth" days for us to understand, not just in our heads but in our hearts, that injustice somewhere is a threat everywhere? How do we convince people of our interconnectedness such that they become activated toward civility? I'd like to learn how to help people to feel the reciprocal links between situations abroad and situations at home. Not long ago, there was another devastating hurricane in Haiti. The country was rendered largely uninhabitable. Thousands of Haitians came to the United States. Some were whipped by border guards on horseback, and the optics harkened back to the days of slavery. Thousands of these migrants were immediately deported back to their uninhabitable country. This occurred not under the Trump administration but under the Biden administration. Oh my God! How inhumane! I know that deportation was what the strict reading of the law dictated, but can we blame homeless and virtually nationless people for seeking shelter? Where was the *active* compassion of the American Buddhists who so often talk about compassion? Perhaps it was muffled by our fear.

———

Dr. King, we have an issue facing us now that was not in our collective awareness when you were alive. Some call it global warming, some call it climate change, others call it climate catastrophe—the point is, our industrialized way of life has emitted so much carbon dioxide and other "greenhouse gases" that they have built up to concentrations that trap enormous amounts of heat in the atmosphere and set off dangerous feedback loops such as melting glaciers and rising sea levels. Earth is hotter than it was when you were here, and consequently, water sources are drying up, huge numbers of species are in danger of extinction, storms are more violent and more frequent, crops don't carry the nourishment they once had, and millions of people are leaving their homes in search of places where they and their families can survive. You had a dream, and we have a nightmare. I share all of this to convey that Buddhist leaders are confronted not only by familiar social challenges but also by ominous environmental challenges that are all but certain to worsen over time. I wonder what you would say to us to help us draw strength and responsiveness from our spiritual, ethical, and religious commitments.

Certain Buddhist leaders, such as His Holiness the Dalai Lama, the late Thich Nhat Hanh, Joanna Macy, Roshi Joan Halifax, Dekila Chungyalpa of the Loka Initiative, and Kristin Barker and the other people at One Earth Sangha (to name a few) have been strong environmental advocates. I have been and remain encouraged by Buddhist Peace Fellowship, Zen Peacemaker Order and Zen Peacemaker International, and other Buddhist-informed activist organizations. Yet I see that Buddhist teachings, and teachings from other religions, can just as easily—perhaps more easily—be used to encourage passivity. I know that you know this all too well. Based on my report about the state of this country, do you think it is time for something like a Buddhist Leadership Conference, something akin to the Southern Christian Leadership Conference (SCLC)? I think the medicine we could offer politicans is the wisdom of the Middle Way. I'm guessing you know something about this, for why else would you have nominated Thich Nhat Hanh for a Nobel Peace Prize? On the question of peacemaking, however, there is something in your letter that concerns me—your reference to the Book of Revelation.

Many Christians turn to the Book of Revelation as if it is a credible divination of what is to come before Jesus returns to claim his people who will live forever. Buddhists and Christians share many beliefs concerning ethics, love, compassion, generosity, and other topics, but one point of divergence is divination. Western Buddhists tend not to believe anyone has the power to predict the future, and we also tend to feel that dwelling in futuristic thinking about existential issues leads to missing the amelioration of suffering that can happen in the here and now. Having experienced both kinds of consciousnesses, I prefer healing in the here and now. I can feel the relief of that orientation, and I know that dreading the future only exacerbates how I feel right now. Having read and contemplated the Jesus depicted in the Gospels and the Jesus depicted in a man's dream in the Book of Revelation, I reject the Revelation Jesus. The Jesus who died on the cross asking God to forgive his persecutors cannot be the same Jesus who returns to destroy 99.9 percent of all who have ever lived, right?

The earth is in a climate crisis, and some of the damage is irreversible. Additional damage can be prevented if we drastically change our ways of life, radically reducing our dependence on industries that produce greenhouse gases. Those who believe in the nightmarish divination in the Book of Revelation have no incentive to support the radical changes we need to make. In fact, many such people oppose all governmental interventions because they believe these actions are futile or that they go against God's prerogative to create and destroy. Above all, they believe that Jesus's return is a fulfillment of the Christian narrative, and letting our way of life fall to pieces is what is supposed to happen just before Jesus's return. I am inspired by your willingness to engage Christian pastors in theological reflection on racism and resistance, and I want to ask you: How do we work on anti-racism projects in this situation of climate change?

Another point of divergence between Christians and Buddhists is that Buddhists do not want to live forever, at least that's what we say. This derives from the classical South Asian worldview in which life is seen as full of suffering. Nevertheless, Mahayana Buddhists hold that if, after we die, we are fortunate to be born human again (as opposed to being reborn in another form), we can live our future lives for the relief of the suffering of others. We call this the bodhisattva aspiration, like being a human angel. With a bodhisattva aspiration, we can also try to be angels on earth, right now—a sort of heaven on earth, if you will. Although you are a Christian, you came to know and respect the

Vietnamese Buddhist monk Thich Nhat Hanh, whom you nominated for a Nobel Peace Prize. (He lived a long, distinguished life and passed away in 2022 at the age of ninety-five.) So perhaps you already know about bodhisattvas, including how they perfect the character trait of determination (among others). I would love to have a conversation with you on these and many other topics. Though I cannot, I hope I can bring some part of your voice and spirit into the conversation with Buddhist leaders alive today.

My dear Buddhist leaders of all races,

I know deep down inside that we are humanitarians, but I challenge us to come forward more consistently in that way. I ask you: How do bodhisattvas preserve the determination for enlightenment? And, how do bodhisattvas preserve the determination for enlightenment *without discrimination*? What role do we play in replacing the bloody garlands with fragrant Avatamsaka flowers? What role do we play in helping others do the same? How do we support each other in Indra's Net such that we amplify our efforts and the consequences of our efforts in practical and mystical ways?

I write to you from the freedom of the three-unit Chicago condo where I live, in which one unit is occupied by a single white man and the other by a white and Indian interracial couple. We share a yard, garage, and garbage and recycling bins. We negotiate home repairs together and share those expenses. Our building is situated next door to another white and Indian interracial couple with interracial children, and next to them is an Asian American couple with a child. On the other side of our building is a Filipino neighbor, and next to his building is a Hispanic family. We live in appreciation for each other as neighbors with absolutely no strife. Period. But that is not how all people in Chicago are living, for Chicago is also notorious for racially segregated communities and gun violence. Nevertheless, I am able to write to you, Buddhist leaders, from a place of freedom, and I am grateful to the civil rights movement for this privilege. Are you?

Like Dr. King's disappointment with many of his good-hearted white Christian pastors, I am also disappointed in many of the good-hearted white Buddhist leaders who talk, write, hold retreats, and counsel practitioners on the liberation that comes from knowing suffering and the end of suffering, but who actively shut POC down when they speak on the causes and conditions of suffering, including the suffering they endure caused by what I'm calling white existential aggravation. Although I'm sure very few or no white Buddhist leaders today would espouse openly white supremacist ideas such as replacement theory—the idea of the white race being "replaced" by black and brown races—I sense that it would be worth your time and effort to examine something that is akin to replacement theory: the dread of the loss of white entitlement and an anticipatory grief-turned-terror. This insecurity, aggravation, dread, and terror keeps changing form, name, and intensity but remains a familiar threat. And this is true despite the consistent "whack-a-moling" by people like Sojourner Truth, George Washington Carver, W.E.B. DuBois, Marian Anderson, Jesse Owens, Joe Louis, Cesar Chavez, Bruce Lee, Muhammad Ali, Barack and Michelle Obama, Yo-Yo Ma, Venus and Serena Williams, Deb Haaland, and countless other mirrors, jewels, and pearls in the Net. After a rich conversation with Buddhist practitioners of many backgrounds at the Future of American Buddhism Conference, I'm ready to set aside the vernacular use of "white supremacy" in favor of "white existential aggravation," by which I mean the reality of white fear, dukkha, and transhistorical karmic fear and projection. These deep-seated feelings have nothing to do with reality but much to do with the cover of the delusion of the lie and the samsara of white supremacy rhetoric that informs policies in need of critical race theory (CRT) as well as the preemptive mass shootings of people of color that beg for anti-racist gun reform, and all forms of hatred in between. This is the complicated reality we need to speak to as the complex multiracial collective that we are.

Rev. Dr. Martin Luther King Jr. used a concept akin to Indra's Net to explain his understanding of our interrelatedness and his concern for the well-being of others, no matter where on earth he was located and no matter where on earth the suffering was being inflicted. Did King, a Christian, get Indra's Net better than we do? King suggested to fellow Christian pastors that they would not be satisfied with a "superficial kind of social analysis that deals merely with effects and does not grapple with underlying causes."[3] As people who believe in "causes and conditions," Buddhist leaders say we want to know why something is as it is. But if that "why" includes POC and our suffering, white leaders collectively shut down, shut off, and consequently shut up people who want to speak of their pain and suffering caused by racism. Compassion, equanimity, lovingkindness, and sympathetic joy are heavenly abodes because they promote the selflessness needed to advocate for others in distress. What more do we need to walk our talk?

We say that one of the ways to heal suffering is through Right Action, not No Action (though sometimes that is also required). True commitment to Right Action may require that we become interested in deeper levels of social analysis that reveal the causes and conditions of suffering. I saw a brilliant presentation on social analysis by Bhikkhu Bodhi at the 2021 International Western Dharma Teachers Gathering. If you haven't seen the presentation, I encourage you to request it. Upon seeing such causes and conditions of hatred clearly, our Buddhist ethical obligation is to contemplate the skillful means to heal the harm while carrying no intention to harm others. This is what nonviolent Right Action is about. According to King, nonviolent action is supported by four basic steps: (1) fact collection to determine whether injustices exist; (2) negotiation with those causing injustice; (3) self-purification; and then (4) direct action. The Buddhist way of nonviolent actions seems to start with (3) self-purification and end with (3) self-purification. If that is true, what are we really doing, and why? It appears we have an inclination toward self-absorption and disconnection. If so, could this be why those involved in nonviolent campaigns tend not to reach out to Buddhist leaders? Are we largely irrelevant to the movements for social change?

Clearly, Buddhist purification as it is practiced today in the West is different from the purification that King wrote about. Kingian self-purification involves repeatedly asking ourselves if we are able to receive physical violence without retaliating. Can we endure being imprisoned? It involves asking these questions, then role-playing to arrive at the answer. This kind of more active, sacrificing purification is not foreign to Buddhism. In the Simile of the Saw Sutta, for instance, the Buddha admonishes his monastics to train so as to maintain lovingkindness practice even if they were to be carved up by bandits limb by limb. He says that if they are attacked, they should remember that the murderous one has the potential to be otherwise and should be reminded of their potential not to be harmful. I see this as the essence of self-purification practice, but today we Buddhists are not role-playing being attacked, practicing lovingkindness in the role play, and preparing to be imprisoned—we are a privileged bunch living off the fruits of the civil rights movement. In my twenty-plus years of practicing Buddhism, no Buddhist has ever asked me to engage in such role plays, and I don't believe I have ever asked anyone to do so, not as a Buddhist practice. Should we engage in nonviolent martial arts as part of our Buddhist practice to embody the teachings? I think so. Also at the Future of American Buddhism Conference, I saw a presentation by the Zen priest Cristina Moon from Daihonzan Chozen-ji, a practice center that has brought the martial and fine arts into its body-centered approach to Zen. She invited researchers to consider doing work on the fact that the historical Buddha was a warrior. I support her invitation one hundred percent.

I've been in Buddhist communities that are helpful for learning about Buddhist thought, philosophy, and practice, but I have not been in the right Buddhist communities for the practices of self-purification as training to absorb harm and prepare for imprisonment. However, the Fourteen Mindfulness Trainings taught in Thich Nhat Hanh's Order of Interbeing are a robust Buddhist basis for nonviolent social activism and could be interpreted in the context of Kingian self-purification. Below, the Fourteen Mindfulness Trainings are given in shortened form for the sake of space.[4]

THE FOURTEEN MINDFULNESS TRAININGS
(FIRST LINES ONLY)

The First Mindfulness Training
Openness
Aware of the suffering created by fanaticism and intolerance, we are determined not to be idolatrous about or bound to any doctrine, theory, or ideology, even Buddhist ones.

The Second Mindfulness Training
Non-attachment to Views
Aware of the suffering created by attachment to views and wrong perceptions, we are determined to avoid being narrow-minded and bound to present views.

The Third Mindfulness Training
Freedom of Thought
Aware of the suffering brought about when we impose our views on others, we are determined not to force others, even our children, by any means whatsoever—such as authority, threat, money, propaganda, or indoctrination—to adopt our views.

The Fourth Mindfulness Training
Awareness of Suffering
Aware that looking deeply at the nature of suffering can help us develop understanding and compassion, we are determined to come home to ourselves, to recognize, accept, embrace, and listen to our own suffering with the energy of mindfulness.

The Fifth Mindfulness Training
Compassionate, Healthy Living
Aware that true happiness is rooted in peace, solidity, freedom, and compassion, we are determined not to accumulate wealth while millions are hungry and dying nor to take as the aim of our life fame, power, wealth, or sensual pleasure, which can bring much suffering and despair.

The Sixth Mindfulness Training
Taking Care of Anger

Aware that anger blocks communication and creates suffering, we are committed to taking care of the energy of anger when it arises, and to recognizing and transforming the seeds of anger that lie deep in our consciousness.

The Seventh Mindfulness Training
Dwelling Happily in the Present Moment

Aware that life is available only in the present moment, we are committed to training ourselves to live deeply in each moment of daily life. We will try not to lose ourselves in dispersion or be carried away by regrets about the past, worries about the future, or craving, anger, or jealousy in the present.

The Eighth Mindfulness Training
True Community and Communication

Aware that lack of communication always brings separation and suffering, we are committed to training ourselves in the practice of compassionate listening and loving speech.

The Ninth Mindfulness Training
Truthful and Loving Speech

Aware that words can create happiness or suffering, we are committed to learning to speak truthfully, lovingly, and constructively. We will use only words that inspire joy, confidence, and hope as well as promote reconciliation and peace in ourselves and among other people. We will speak and listen in a way that can help ourselves and others to transform suffering and see the way out of difficult situations. We are determined not to say untruthful things for the sake of personal interest or to impress people, nor to utter words that might cause division or hatred. We will protect the happiness and harmony of our sangha by refraining from speaking about the faults of other persons in their absence and always asking ourselves whether our perceptions are correct. We will speak only with the intention to understand and help transform the situation. We will not spread rumors nor criticize or condemn things of which we are not sure. We will do our best to speak out about situations of injustice, *even when doing so may make difficulties for us or threaten our safety.*[5]

The Tenth Mindfulness Training
Protecting and Nourishing the Sangha

Aware that the essence and aim of a sangha is the realization of understanding and compassion, we are determined not to use the Buddhist community for personal power or profit, or transform our community into a political instrument. As members of a spiritual community, *we should nonetheless take a clear stand against oppression and injustice.*[6] We should strive to change the situation, without taking sides in a conflict. We are committed to learning to look with the eyes of interbeing and to see ourselves and others as cells in one sangha body. As a true cell in the sangha body, generating mindfulness, concentration, and insight to nourish ourselves and the whole community, each of us is at the same time a cell in the Buddha body. We will actively build brotherhood and sisterhood, flow as a river, and practice to develop the three real powers—understanding, love, and cutting through afflictions—to realize collective awakening.

The Eleventh Mindfulness Training
Right Livelihood

Aware that great violence and injustice have been done to our environment and society, we are committed not to live with a vocation that is harmful to humans and nature.

The Twelfth Mindfulness Training
Reverence for Life

Aware that much suffering is caused by war and conflict, we are determined to cultivate nonviolence, compassion, and the insight of interbeing in our daily lives and promote peace education, mindful mediation, and reconciliation within families, communities, ethnic and religious groups, nations, and in the world.

The Thirteenth Mindfulness Training
Generosity

Aware of the suffering caused by exploitation, social injustice, stealing, and oppression, we are committed to cultivating generosity in our way of thinking, speaking, and acting.

The Fourteenth Mindfulness Training
True Love

[For lay members]: Aware that sexual desire is not love and that sexual relations motivated by craving cannot dissipate the feeling of loneliness but will create more suffering, frustration, and isolation, we are determined not to engage in sexual relations without mutual understanding, love, and a deep long-term commitment made known to our family and friends. Seeing that body and mind are not separate from each other, we are committed to learning appropriate ways to take care of our sexual energy and to cultivating lovingkindness, compassion, joy, and inclusiveness for our own happiness and the happiness of others.

Buddhist leaders of all lineages, I ask you to seriously contemplate the ninth and tenth trainings. What arises for you in these contemplations? In the context of the "democratic authoritarianism" that is a growing threat in the United States, how will we show up differently?

Dear Rev. Dr. King,

The Fourteen Mindfulness Trainings were written in 1966. They remind me of what attracted me to Thich Nhat Hanh's teachings in his book *Touching Peace*. Given that you nominated him for the Nobel Peace Prize in 1967, you must have known how deeply meaningful and positively transformative his teachings were when you were alive together. When you nominated him, he had written ten books. Would you believe he cofounded Parallax Press in 1986, and he and his editors penned more than one hundred books? Being the theologian you are, I know you would be impressed!

As I reread these trainings, I wonder if you noticed what I noticed this time at the end of the ninth and the beginning of the tenth training. At the end of the ninth, it is written, "We will do our best to speak out about situations of injustice, even when doing so may make difficulties for us or threaten our safety." As you and all the other named and unnamed activists who kept the civil rights movement in motion know, it takes incredible courage to speak out about situations of injustice at the cost of personal difficulty and danger. It still takes incredible courage in the current iteration of the civil rights movement, which some call Black Lives Matter. But then at the beginning of the tenth training, it says, "Aware that the essence and aim of a sangha is the practice of understanding and compassion, we are determined not to use the Buddhist community for personal power or profit, or transform our community into a political instrument. As members of a spiritual community, we should nonetheless take a clear stand against oppression and injustice. We should strive to change the situation, without taking sides in a conflict." Rev. Dr. King, how does a spiritual community take a clear stand against oppression and injustice without becoming a political instrument?

The church is used as a political instrument for supporting political candidates who sometimes support policies and laws that create systems of injustice—this is especially so in the hands of some evangelical Christians involved in policy- and law-making. I understand something about the danger of openly taking a side from reading Sister Chan Khong's book *Learning True Love*. She writes that doing so causes the side not taken to perceive you as an enemy. Yet moral or immoral equivalency, I think, is part of what keeps Buddhist practitioners stuck in cultivating insight and compassion in a context of inaction rather than taking insight and compassion into nonviolent Right Action. What advice do you have for us that will support us being witnesses and advocates, and also inform us as to when we are being used as political pawns so that we can reject political exploitation?

Also, you may have noticed that there is nothing in these truly wonderful mindfulness trainings that prepares us to receive the blows of violence without retaliation. That aspect of self-purification is at least not explicit in the trainings, but adding teachings from the Simile of the Saw could be instructive. I think we Buddhist leaders need to develop role plays such as your movement did and teach people in our communities to do the same. Thank you, Rev. Dr. King, for your life and the opportunity to correspond with your invoked spirit. May you continue to rest in peace and power.

Dear White Buddhist Leaders,

How does it feel to be invested in a culture and practice that remains largely irrelevant to solving the white existential threats to people of color? This question came to mind as I reread and contemplated Dr. Martin Luther King Jr.'s "Letter from Birmingham Jail." In this 1963 letter, he asks his fellow Christian pastors, those who criticized non-violent direct action to end racial segregation, to understand his perspective and get involved in the movement.

Fast forward nearly sixty years. Did you live through the Trump administration? If so, what did you see? How do you feel about the fact that the former president—twice impeached; who led the separation of children from their immigrant parents; who was in part responsible for the deaths of thousands due to his COVID-19 denials; who was the instigator of a deadly coup attempt on January 6, 2021; and who is a white nationalist himself—still "leads" the "Republican" party and has millions of supporters? Whether there is a second Trump administration or not, the former Republican Party has capitulated to lawlessness, alternative realities, conspiracy theories, and authoritarianism. What do you think this will mean for people of color? Let us not forget that a whistleblower blew the top off of the secret sterilizations of immigrant women by US governmental medical professionals at Irwin County Detention Center in Georgia. Oh my God! Isn't it interesting how people can be "right to life" supporters and ignore forced sterilization? Will we hold our political leaders accountable for committing crimes against humanity? Dharma teachers, how can we teach about liberation and freedom and not be actively addressing these concerns in sangha and elsewhere? There are

Zen and Buddhist leaders sticking their necks out on behalf of the rest of us. Let's join them.

There is a quote in Rev. Dr. King's letter where he talks about being black and parenting a black child who wants to do something that white people are permitted to do, but black people are banned from. He asks white people to understand the psychological development of black children "and see ominous clouds of inferiority beginning to form in [their] little mental sky, and see [them] beginning to distort [their] personality by developing an unconscious bitterness toward white people."[7] Today, we are no longer living in the de jure racially segregated context we used to live in, but many of us still have reasons to be bitter. Can you understand that? Can you make a place in your sangha for healing the bitterness caused by racial harm without taking it personally? Are you willing to see how the racial context of our society puts you at risk of developing a superiority complex and bitterness toward people of color, and that if you enter and remain in such states, you will be unable to mirror, twin, and reflect our pain, suffering, and humanity?

In this age of Black Lives Matter racial reckoning, a cultural phenomenon formed and is currently called "Karen." "Karen" is a name used to label a white woman bent on putting black people in subordinate places based on deluded thoughts of an innate criminality and uppityness within the black psyche. The #BLM movement to expose this trend, which raised its head repeatedly during the Trump years, was very successful in exposing the ways some white women use their aggression, or white rage (read Carol Anderson's book by the same title), to attempt to keep black people in check. I believe the success of calling out "Karen" helped stimulate another form of white rage—the nationwide attack on critical race theory. CRT was coined and developed in the mid-1970s by legal scholars, including the Harvard Law School professor Derrick Bell, Kimberlé Crenshaw, Cheryl Harris, Richard Delgado, Patricia Williams, Gloria Ladson-Billings, Tara Yosso, and others. In King's letter, which came years before CRT, he wrote:

> Let us consider a more concrete example of just and unjust laws. An unjust law is a code that a numerical or power majority group compels a minority group to obey but does not make binding on itself. This is difference made legal. By the same token, a just law is a code that a majority compels a minority to follow and that is willing to follow itself. This is sameness made legal."[8]

Those who attack CRT attack the spirit of Rev. Dr. Martin Luther King Jr. and the civil rights movement, but there is no real hurt there. The real hurt is being done to school children, especially white children. When I was a freshman in college in 1980 (twenty-six years after school racial segregation was found to be unconstitutional), I sat next to Susan, a white woman-child from Alabama. Susan told me that she had never sat next to a black person until she sat next to me in the cafeteria. I found that remarkable in 1980. One day, we watched *To Kill a Mockingbird* in the dorm with other students. Susan became distraught because the film challenged everything her father had told her about the relationship between black and white people in the US. He told her that white people had always been kind to black people and that Yankees had told lies about Southerners and slavery. After the movie ended, Susan told me she was going to confront her father, and she did.

If we want our children to trust us (and I hope we do), we should tell them the truth about our history, and we should prepare them for reality so they develop the ability to live life as it is. The quest for real freedom and real liberation always requires criticality on matters pertaining to law and its potentially enslaving impacts. I know Rev. Dr. King would not be surprised by the pushback against public school children learning about racism in the United States. Maybe he'd even see this current form of racism as a manifestation of his dream becoming a reality, for he never said that once our children walk hand in hand, their parents (we) would suddenly not be threatened by the cross-cultural alliances our fierce children are making, like when they repeatedly marched throughout this country after George Floyd was tortured and murdered. It appears that Karens are avenging the fact they have been successfully called out, and they are taking their rage out on school boards. Yes, school boards and teachers! The "crime" being committed is teachers offering lessons on racism. Oh my God! I heard a white parent say that she opposed CRT because it teaches her child that she, the parent, is a racist. I know that is not what CRT is about, so I feel sad when I hear parents get worked up over something that isn't true. What is true about CRT? Here are a few of its core positions:

- Recognition that race is not biologically real but is socially constructed and socially significant.
- Acknowledgment that racism is a normal feature of society and is embedded within systems and institutions, like the legal system, that replicates racial inequality.
- Racism is codified in law, embedded in structures, and woven into public policy. It is the systemic nature of racism that bears primary responsibility for reproducing racial inequality.
- Recognition of the relevance of people's everyday lives to scholarship. This includes embracing the lived experiences of

people of color, including those preserved through storytelling, and rejecting deficit-informed research that excludes the epistemologies of people of color.[9]

Buddhist philosophy and ontology support viewing race as a social construction. The police torture and murder of many unarmed black people remind us that racism is supported by legal systems to perpetuate a society based on the delusion of separateness, but Buddhist leaders have often balked at the notion of amplifying the lived experience of people of color. Why? Many white Buddhist leaders are probably sympathetic with what I call Karen Revenge, but why? I believe cultural conditioning by the trope that white women are innately fragile, coupled with white men's need to be powerful and needed by white women, and the interlocking of these delusions and needs contributes to racism in another form—anti-CRT activism.

Buddhist leaders say we are about truth. The truth is people of color have been subjugated for centuries, and we're still rebelling, re-creating, envisioning, and building something new. It is anathema to Buddhism to deny these facts. Buddhist leaders, it is time again to stand up, speak out for truth, and work in solidarity for the lived experience of liberation.

AFFIRMATION
I invoke the spirit of spiritual guides

The memory, history, and story of people who have done good in this world can be invoked in your meditation practice. Bring them to mind when you sit. I invoke the spirit of spiritual guides.

Conclusion

Civility as Spiritual Practice and Public Pastoral Care

Living in the network of our mutuality and brutality comes with responsibilities and opportunities. There are so many belief systems, customs, languages, and cultures. Such pluralism can be dizzying, confounding, and anxiety-producing on a relational level, enticing many of us to stick with the familiarity and comfort of our clan.

I accompany people on their spiritual journeys as a spiritual director, chaplain, and pastoral counselor, and I have chosen to work in pluralistic contexts, including the public square, without disqualifying people based simply on their religious or spiritual beliefs. Nevertheless, I still remain extremely limited in my understanding of various beliefs because I have no long-term lived experience of most belief systems. Consequently, I, like many of us, have been confused by what I've learned about certain belief systems and the people affiliated with them. For instance, when my partner and I were preparing for our backyard wedding and reception, we contemplated whether we should invite our wonderful neighbor Susan (a different Susan than the one from college), a Mormon. We lived across the street from the

Mormon Temple, and we lived next door to the house occupied by the temple caretakers. We had no problem being neighbors to Mormons, and they were always friendly toward us. We had no problem with our child playing with Susan's children, and the children enjoyed each other. But what would it mean to invite Susan to a same-sex wedding, especially when her church heavily invested in anti-same-sex-marriage campaigns? After some contemplation, I called Susan and asked if I could speak with her. As we sat at her kitchen table, I felt the familiar tension throughout my body as I prepared myself to be rejected again. I remember saying something about the Mormon stance on same-sex marriage and continuing to say that I wanted to invite her to the wedding but would understand if she would not accept our invitation. I nervously offered the invitation and paused. Susan began to cry, and I jumped to the conclusion that I had indeed made a terrible mistake. I apologized but soon learned that no apology was necessary. Susan told me that she cried because so many people had judged her as being narrow-minded, anti-gay, anti-woman, anti-others, all because she was a Mormon. She went on to tell me about her Mormon mother's feminist activism within the church and that she inherited her mother's philosophy and work. She told me about her own life in China, why she chose to teach English as a second language, and she shared her care for me and my partner.

When she was done, I broke down. We cried together. Susan accepted our invitation, and having her at our wedding and our other Mormon neighbors at our reception meant the world to us. It is because of experiences like these that I, as a spiritual caregiver in the plurality of our world, remain committed to interreligious curiosity and appreciation as I actively work through the samsara of interreligious ignorance. I find it all fascinating, juicy, and fulfilling!

Over and over again, especially if our appetite for authoritarianism grows, we will all be invited to use our ignorance of each other against each other. For example, Islamophobia is deep within the United States's collective body and consciousness, especially after 9/11, the twenty-year Afghanistan War, and the anti-Muslim travel ban. Other countries and regions divided by religious identities also harbor their own religious phobias. In the United States context, I ask non-Muslims to protect themselves from a deepening Islamophobia by simply opening the Qu'ran. The first time I opened a Qu'ran was when I was a Zen Hospice Project volunteer. Zen and Islam? Delicious! A Muslim who was dying wanted someone to read it to him. I did it without hesitation because of his request. Years later, when I taught an interreligious chaplaincy course at a Christian seminary, I invited students to experiment with a form of Muslim prayer, and one student refused. It was his loss as well as the loss of Muslims he might minister to. The embodied, felt-sense similarities between the form of Muslim prayer and yoga were so striking to me that I wondered why yoga (unity) is so embraced in our culture, yet not the physical prayers of unity in Islam? I invite you to wonder with me, for the time will come again and again for us to show up in solidarity with people engaging in the responsible practices of their religious freedom, including showing solidarity with the many Muslims who are also engaging their religious freedoms responsibly. One way we can do this is to make space for our kin, to tell our shared stories, and to model solidarity. This is the reason why I asked author Eboo Patel, an American Muslim and founder of Interfaith America, to have the last word in this book. We are all in the inescapable net of mutuality and brutality. We have the opportunity to cast our nets to retrieve the abundance already present while also polishing our reflective selves for the benefit of people seeing themselves as they truly are.

Of necessity, we experience Indra's Net from our own perspective, and this can easily lead to delusions of a separate self. But the Net is not controlled by a single individual. We can all cast it. How we deal with this reality can produce a host of negative emotion and, eventually, chaos and brutality. We have shown we can collect all that brutal energy into mobbery. For many of us, feelings of economic inadequacy have been exploited, interpreted as something to be ashamed of, and justified as a reason for acting with brutality against each other. Americans across the political spectrum are subject to pressures of polarization and group anger, and these pressures are likely to intensify as we move deeper into the era of climate change and mass migration. On the other hand, living in the inescapable network of our mutuality is a constant and dynamic opportunity to transform brutality. What part do you want to play? I believe we must strive to be less susceptible to rageful exploitation because we know its pointlessness.

Civility can be not only a part of our spiritual practice but also an offering of public pastoral care. This practice involves regulating and managing our emotions and behavior, as well as cultivating our intelligence. The US Constitution is an organizing and living document that we need to read and reread so as to orient and reorient ourselves toward freedom and justice. We would do well to reconsider the role of each branch of government and the military because they each have responsibilities to protect us and can also be used against us. If we don't strengthen these systems in the best ways possible, we will continue the trend toward vigilantism.

We are becoming a culture of mobbery over respect for the rule of law. Yet our interdependent reality remains ripe with ethical opportunities. We have within us, still, the innate mutuality we were born into. We each have a lei around our necks and, with civility and hospitality, we can adorn it with many fragrant flowers. If we remember the reasons why we should bow to one another, surrendering to our vulnerability, paradoxically that will actually level us up to positions of greater self-esteem. Unfortunately though, we have been adding more bloody fingers to our garlands, and people are being hurt, maimed, and murdered in the deluded interest of profoundly insecure people struggling with narcissism. I believe such people can find the path to releasing their clinging to perceived insignificance, and I hope they will do so. Ultimately, mobbery crushes our spiritual lives. Yet, I remain an optimist about human potential because I understand the power of contemplation to return us to our original mutuality.

We have encountered different types of contemplation in this book, including meditations and making and reflecting on ethical commitments. An additional type of contemplation, which I undertook in the previous chapter in my letters to Rev. Dr. King, is to recognize wise and compassionate people (dead or alive) and ask them questions. This is called "invoking the spirit"—an indigenous way of knowing. This practice places us in a position of healthy humility and receptiveness to the wisdom of people who were or are more spiritually mature than we are. Transmuting our narcissistic tendencies requires that we rely on others, and how wonderful it is that we can engage our imaginations and ancestral connections in doing so. Are you willing to identify wise people and ask them how they embarked on their wisdom path, what they surrendered along the way, how they practice determination, how they cultivate curiosity about awakening, how they practice deep meditative states, and what liberation is really all about? If you know no one you can talk to, then talk to the ancestors who have left us the legacy of their wisdom. Step into your inheritance.

As we continue to have these contemplations and engagements in wise dialogue with sages, I believe we will come to better appreciate the teachings on selflessness and generosity. It seems clear to me that we need to transcend old slogans like the Golden Rule that may be ineffective, or at least not enough, for our pluralistic society. Even for those who seek to abide by the Golden Rule, too often our narcissism leads us to impose our unwanted self-template on others. If we avoid the real challenges of dialogue across difference and only expect others to treat us as we want to be treated, that usually means being treated with a politeness that avoids conflict, confrontation, intimacy, deep curiosity, and creativity.

In the introduction to this book, I asked if it is time for a compassion *revolution*. Compassion, in essence, means to suffer with others. Many wisdom traditions teach compassion through a variety of stories and methods, and I hope that the stories we've explored in this book have illuminated the topic from various angles. The Buddha, Angulimala, and other Buddhist seekers; Jesus, the Canaanite woman, and the lawyer who asked Jesus about neighborliness; Job; Arjuna—all had questions pertaining to the ethics of living together. Why not ask some questions yourself? Pursuing life without asking questions is like living in community with disunity, and the arrogance of believing we know everything we need to know clouds our mirrors, diamonds, and pearls, dimming the brightness of our reflection. We can thus become dull, and people notice it—even dull people notice there is no use in bringing a dull person their suffering. Dullness begets dullness. As Jesus said in the Book of Luke, let the dead bury the dead. Why not be the shining star you really are? In terms of practice, contemplation, prayer, meditation, and service are other ways to cultivate compassion. Listening deeply to those in despair, empathizing, entering the realm of interpathy, and not denying our feelings when we do, can give rise to compassionate responses.

Compassion means to suffer with others, yet we need nuance in our approach to being with others. In the rising tide of mobbery, compassionate action also involves renouncing the intention to harm and refraining from gathering to perform acts of collective aggression and existential aggravation. If we are to collaborate creatively to find our place in the world, relying on one another's strengths and contributing our own, we will need to improve our ability to live in the inescapable Net. We were conceived into the Net, born into it, and exist within it. We will die in its entanglements. In the meantime, can we enhance the ways we live in this vast and abundant community of kin, near and far?

Being the shining star you really are is living into the undeniable knowing of your place in the cosmos. You and every other star in the universe have a right to be here until your light goes out. Knowing we have a place in the cosmos helps us to not be stagnant in Indra's Net but rather to fortify it. By that I mean we affirm and reaffirm our resilience, the non-anxious presence we need to extend our cosmic hospitality. Through shining our mirror, diamond, and pearl-like selves for the benefit of others, so that they can see their own mirror, diamond, and pearl-like selves when they look at us. We become better able to do this because we have done our work (turning our gold into platinum) to love ourselves as we love others, to create heaven on earth, to be on the long pilgrimage to see each other as kin, just as El-Hajj Malik El-Shabazz (Malcolm X) did on his pilgrimage to Mecca. To recognize our belonging to others and their belonging to us, just as Thomas Merton did on his stay-pilgrimage on a street corner in Louisville, Kentucky. Our survival depends on short- and long-term, informal and formal adoption of each other across our real and perceived differences. We can be play cousins for each other.

For me, the truest nature of love is felt. Trying to stay alive during the COVID-19 pandemic has meant we've had to physically separate ourselves from many others. I believe the lack of the felt sense of community has had a negative impact on the way we cognize (think about) others at a distance. The felt sense of love cannot be perfectly produced just by words. If you are like me, you will feel loved by someone when:

- They look you in the eye and smile.
- They are mostly quiet as they listen to you.
- They are curious about what you feel and how you experience life.
- They wish no harm to you.
- They wish the best for you.
- They have a desire to help you when you are in need, even if they cannot really help you.
- They encourage you to help yourself because they really believe you have the capability to do so.
- They show hospitality.
- They apologize when they get it all wrong.

And when we do this for others, we strengthen the Net.

AFFIRMATION

I reflect the basic goodness of everyone I meet

Polishing my mirror, shining my diamonds, and buffing my pearls, I twin and reflect the basic goodness of everyone I meet and receive the reflections of those who have done the same. I reflect the basic goodness of everyone I meet.

Afterword

This beautiful book brings me back—back to the time when I was an angry college activist looking for a different way. I knew the world was full of injustice and needed change, but the path of rage that I had been on for my first two years as an activist was not sustainable. It was burning me up inside.

And then somebody said a short sentence that changed my life: "Have you ever heard of Dorothy Day?"

Reading the work of Dorothy Day and spending time with the Catholic Worker movement initiated me into a new way of being a social change agent. Activism is about loving people, not hating the system. Social change is about building things up, not burning things down.

Reading Ayo Yetunde's book brought me back to that paradigm-shifting moment in my life.

There is such wisdom in this text. It questions whether we as a human species are going to choose brutality or mutuality and whether we'll celebrate and commit to the "wholeworking" of community building rather than merely settling for the "networking" of career advancement.

I love the stories that Ayo shares about her Buddhist faith practice. The most powerful one for me was the tale of how she went from being someone deeply uncomfortable with death and funerals to a spiritual partner and chaplain who accompanies people on their journey of dying. Faith can work miracles in our lives.

I also love the social vision of this book. Buddhism is often wrongly viewed as a religion that focuses only on the inward journey of self. But Ayo shows in this book that there is a deep connection between becoming a healthy, whole self and helping the world become healthy and whole. Ayo herself has made this connection in practical ways, by embracing Buddhist silence as a spiritual practice and also by enacting a kind of Buddhist "standing up" in her work founding the Buddhist Justice Reporter publication.

I want to thank Ayo for this lovely text. I think of it as a contribution to Interfaith America—the chapter of American history that I believe we are in or, more accurately, that we are starting to write. But Ayo's vision, I suspect, is even larger. She would say that this is a stitch in the fabric of Interfaith World.

—Eboo Patel, founder and president of Interfaith America
and author of *We Need to Build* and *Acts of Faith*

Notes

Introduction
Finding Our Place in the Network of Mutuality

1. Martin Luther King Jr. "The Three Dimensions of a Complete Life," in *Letter from Birmingham Jail* (London: Penguin Books UK, 2018), 42–43.
2. https://www.buddhistjustice.com/.
3. Martin Luther King Jr. "Remaining Awake Through a Great Revolution," commencement address for Oberlin College, June 1965, https://www2.oberlin.edu/external/EOG/BlackHistoryMonth /MLK/CommAddress.html.
4. J. Rosamond Johnson and James Weldon Johnson, "Lift Every Voice and Sing," https://www.poetryfoundation.org/poems/46549/lift -every-voice-and-sing.

Chapter 1. The Suffering of Mobbery

1. Mary Hui, "White supremacist saved by black protester after being punched at anti-Nazi march," *Independent*, October 23, 2017, https://www.independent.co.uk/news/world/americas/us-politics

/white-supremacist-black-protester-neo-nazi-richard-spencer-florida
-alachua-county-a8015306.html.

2. John Bowden, "Black protester who carried injured white man
wanted to avert 'catastrophe,'" *The Hill*, June 15, 2020, https://thehill
.com/blogs/blog-briefing-room/news/502734-black-protester-who
-carried-injured-white-man-wanted-to-avert.

3. "The Fourteen Mindfulness Trainings," Plum Village, accessed April
29, 2022, https://plumvillage.org/mindfulness-practice/the-14
-mindfulness-trainings/.

Chapter 2. Beyond the Golden Rule: Treating Others as *They Need* to Be Treated

1. Other writers have also written about a Platinum Rule—Tony
Alessandra and Michael O'Connor, for example, have titled a series
of books as such. But their version of the rule, I learned after writing
my chapter on the topic, largely pertains to business personalities and
achieving commercial success. Their definition of their Platinum Rule
differs radically from my own.

2. David. W. Augsburger, *Pastoral Counseling Across Cultures*
(Philadelphia: Westminster Press, 1986), 14.

Chapter 3. The Four Noble Truths as a Path of Mutuality and Relationality

1. Gil Fronsdal, *The Issue at Hand: Essays on Buddhist Mindfulness
Practice* (Boston: Shambhala Publications, 2001), 146.

2. It is important to note here that the use of the word "caste" is
historically and culturally loaded. "Caste" in the context of the
Buddha's time refers to ancient Indian social structures predating
British imperialism. But "caste" also refers to a social mechanism of
British colonial rule in India and throughout the British empire. And
I also use "caste" to signify the intercultural transmission of violent,
imperialistic oppression in the US. My use of this word should not be
misconstrued to suggest I am anti-Hindu people. To the contrary, my

spiritual life has been uplifted by Hindu people, the Gita, and Eknath
Easwaran's series The Bhagavad Gita for Daily Living.

Chapter 5.
The Book of Job: Self-actualization through Community

1. Pierre Tristam, "When the Nation of Islam Leader Embraced True
   Islam and Abandoned Separatism," ThoughtCo, January 17, 2021,
   https://www.thoughtco.com/malcom-x-in-mecca-2353496.
2. Thomas Merton, *Conjectures of a Guilty Bystander* (New York:
   Doubleday, 1965).

Chapter 6. Action without Attachment:
The Bhagavad Gita and the Lessons of Paradox

1. Earth Wind & Fire, "Shining Star," accessed November 7, 2021,
   https://www.azlyrics.com/lyrics/earthwindandfire/shiningstar.html.
2. Stephen Mitchell, ed., *Bhagavad Gita* (New York: Harmony Books,
   2000), 43.
3. Mitchell, *Bhagavad Gita*, 46.
4. Mitchell, 129.
5. Stephen Mitchell, ed., *Tao Te Ching* (New York: Harper and Row,
   1988), 22.
6. Mitchell, *Bhagavad Gita*, 155.
7. Mitchell, 158.
8. Prasiddha Sudhakar, et al., "Quantitative Methods for Investigating
   Anti-Hindu Disinformation," Rutgers Miller Center for Community
   Protection and Resilience. Accessed August 2, 2022, https://network
   contagion.us/wp-content/uploads/NCRI-Anti-Hindu-Disinform
   ation-v2.pdf.
9. Billie Holiday, vocalist, "Strange Fruit," by Abel Meerpool, 1939.
   Accessed December 13, 2021, https://genius.com/Billie-holiday
   -strange-fruit-lyrics.
10. *Merriam-Webster*, s.v. "autonomy (n.)," http://www.merriam-webster
    .com/dictionary/autonomy.

11. Pema Chödrön, *Compassion Cards: Teachings for Awakening the Heart in Everyday Life* (Boulder, CO: Shambhala, 2016). Slogan translations © 1981, 1986 by Diana J. Mukpo; revised translation © 1993 by Diana J. Mukpo and the Nālandā Translation Committee

Chapter 7. Knowing Your Place in the Cosmos

1. Max Ehrmann, "Desiderata," accessed December 16, 2021, https://www.desiderata.com/desiderata.html.

2. "The First Black Woman to Pilot a Spacecraft Says Seeing Earth Was the Best Part," *NPR*, September 14, 2021, https://www.npr.org /transcripts/1040353478.

3. Thomas Merton, *Conjectures of a Guilty Bystander* (New York: Doubleday, 1965), 44–45.

4. "Gatha," *Mindfulness Bell* #23, Winter 1998, https://www.mindful nessbell.org/archive/2016/01/gatha-2.

5. Mitchell, *Tao Te Ching*, 26–27.

Chapter 8. Letters from a Chicago Condo: To Rev. Dr. Martin Luther King Jr. and to My Buddhist Kin

1. Martin Luther King Jr., *Letter from Birmingham Jail* (London: Penguin Books UK, 2018), 3.

2. King, *Letter from Birmingham Jail*, 5.

3. King, 3.

4. Thich Nhat Hanh, *Interbeing*, 4th ed. (Berkeley, CA: Parallax Press). I encourage readers to read the full text of the Fourteen Mindfulness Trainings, which are also available at https://plumvillage.org/mind fulness/the-14-mindfulness-trainings/.

5. Italics added.

6. Italics added.

7. King, *Letter from Birmingham Jail*, 8.

8. King, 11,

9. Janel George, "A Lesson on Critical Race Theory," *American Bar Association*, January 11, 2021, https://www.americanbar.org/groups /crsj/publications/human_rights_magazine_home/civil-rights -reimagining-policing/a-lesson-on-critical-race-theory/.

About the Author

PAMELA AYO YETUNDE, JD, MA, ThD, is a pastoral counselor, spiritual director, chaplain, and Community Dharma Leader in the Insight Meditation community. She is coeditor of the Nautilus Gold Award-winning *Black and Buddhist: What Buddhism Can Teach Us About Race, Resilience, Transformation, and Freedom* (Shambhala Publications, 2020); author of *Object Relations, Buddhism, and Relationality in Womanist Practical Theology* (Palgrave Macmillan, 2018) and the Frederick J. Streng Award-winning *Buddhist-Christian Dialogue, U.S. Law, and Womanist Theology for Transgender Spiritual Care* (Palgrave Macmillan, 2020); and editor of the Theology of Prince Journal (United Theological Seminary of the Twin cities, 2018). Ayo is an associate editor with *Lion's Roar* magazine. Ayo is cofounder of Center of the Heart (www.centeroftheheart.org) and Buddhist Justice Reporter (www.buddhistjustice.com). Ayo has been featured on NBC.com, *The Tamron Hall Show*, and Sisters from AARP. She is the recipient of the Outstanding Women in Buddhism Award by the International Women's Meditation Center Foundation. Ayo's next project is a contemporary rendering of an ancient Buddhist story through story, theater, and film. Pamela Ayo Yetunde can be reached at www.ayoyetunde.com.